STOP THE SCREAMING

Also by Carl Pickhardt and from Palgrave Macmillan

The Future of Your Only Child: How to Guide Your Child to a Happy and Successful Life

The Connected Father: Understanding Your Unique Role and Responsibilities during Your Child's Adolescence

For more books by Carl Pickhardt, see www.carlpickhardt.com

STOP THE SCREAMING

HOW TO TURN ANGRY CONFLICT WITH YOUR CHILD INTO POSITIVE COMMUNICATION

Carl E. Pickhardt, Ph.D.

palgrave
macmillan

STOP THE SCREAMING
Copyright © Carl E. Pickhardt, 2009.

First published in 2009 by
PALGRAVE MACMILLAN®
in the United States—a division of St. Martin's Press LLC,
175 Fifth Avenue, New York, NY 10010.

Where this book is distributed in the UK, Europe and the rest of the world,
this is by Palgrave Macmillan, a division of Macmillan Publishers Limited,
registered in England, company number 785998, of Houndmills,
Basingstoke, Hampshire RG21 6XS.

Palgrave Macmillan is the global academic imprint of the above companies
and has companies and representatives throughout the world.

Palgrave® and Macmillan® are registered trademarks in the United States,
the United Kingdom, Europe and other countries.

ISBN-13: 978–0–230–60645–6
ISBN-10: 0–230–60645–8

Library of Congress Cataloging-in-Publication Data is available from the
Library of Congress.

A catalogue record of the book is available from the British Library.

Design by Newgen Imaging Systems (P) Ltd., Chennai, India.

First edition: January, 2009.

10 9 8 7 6 5 4 3 2 1

Printed in the United States of America.

Shortly before she died at age 97, my stepmother gave me a commission: "Read Heraclitus." And so, like many times before, she set me on another path of understanding: That ancient Greek philosopher is the inspiration for this book, which I dedicate with gratitude to them both.

The poet was a fool who wanted no conflict among us.... From the strain of binding opposites comes harmony.

—Brooks Haxton, *Fragments: The Collected Wisdom of Heraclitus*

Conflict is a natural and even inevitable aspect of most ongoing close relationships. So the issue that differentiates successful from unsuccessful relationships is not whether there is conflict but, rather, how it is handled.

—Daniel J. Canary, William R. Cupach, and Susan J. Messman, *Relationship Conflict*

Though conflict is a human universal, so are efforts to reduce it.

—Steven Pinker, *How the Mind Works*

CONTENTS

DISCLAIMER

Unless otherwise attributed, all quotations and examples in this book are fictional, similar in kind but not in actuality to cases I have known, made up by me to illustrate psychological points.

ACKNOWLEDGMENT

I would like to express my gratitude to Grace Freedson for representing my nonfiction work.

INTRODUCTION

I wrote *Stop the Screaming* in order to help parents better understand and resolve conflicts with their children and adolescents. Not abusive or violent, these are the conflicts that arise in the normal course of family life. They happen at any time or on any occasion—during play, at family meals, and even on vacations. They are typically based on misunderstandings, disagreements, or incompatibilities. *Misunderstandings* can happen when messages are unclear or false assumptions are made. *Disagreements* can happen when perceptions are contradictory or opposing wants collide. *Incompatibilities* can happen when characteristics are not shared or when two people rub each other the wrong way. *Conflict is the process through which individuals confront and work out these kinds of differences in human relationships.*

Several parental roles provoke conflict with children. As *managers* of family life, parents give directions, make rules, demand obedience, and apply consequences. Children may take offense to any or all of these. Because children sometimes resent parental authority, a child may resist: "Why should I have to do what you want?" As *messengers* of bad tidings, parents give opinions, advice, and evaluation, which children may find irritating or overly critical. When the parental point of view is unwelcome, the child may protest: "I don't want to hear what you're saying!" As *mediators* of disputes, parents arbitrate disagreements between siblings. Because it's nearly impossible to come up with a solution that both children consider equitable and just, one child may feel mistreated and object: "You're being unfair!"

Conflict is built into parenthood in other ways as well. When a young child pushes parents for more freedom, parents must restrain that push for independence out of concern for the child's safety. The child protests this parental restraint, creating ongoing conflicts of interest. The frequency and intensity of conflict typically increase during adolescence, when obtaining social freedom becomes an urgent need for the teenager and when allowing social freedom can feel more problematic to parents. In addition, parenting is always a process of playing catch-up. The child develops in unanticipated ways, venturing into uncharted experiences, leaving parents operating under a set of old expectations that do not fit the child's new reality. Conflict results when parents cannot understand and accept that their child is growing older.

No matter how much parent and child love each other, not everything about each other is always going to please, harmoniously match, or mesh. Intermittent conflict between parent and child is simply part of family life, usually taking participants out of their emotional comfort zone with each other until settlement is reached and normalcy is restored. In caring relationships, the emotional discomfort aroused by the disharmony of conflict can be a motivation for avoiding or resolving it.

Although conflict with children is inevitable, parents have significant control over *how* that conflict is managed. They can let it divide and estrange them from the child, or they can treat each conflict as a valuable opportunity. *Conflict becomes a creative process* when, through open discussion, two different ways of looking at a disagreement generate a third view that increases the understanding of both parties, producing a resolution that neither party conceived of before.

When well conducted, conflict between parent and child can increase *intimacy* and *unity* between them. Intimacy is increased when parent and child can discuss a troublesome issue and come to a better understanding of each other. Unity is increased when both parent and child can bridge their disagreement with an arrangement each is willing to accept and honor. Of course, this is often not easy to do.

Talking out and working out disagreements can be difficult because of the tension and frustration involved in family conflict and because the resolution is often based on an agreement that is imperfect for both parties. Consider the example of a high school student who is forbidden to attend a college fraternity party because her parents believe she is too young. The teenager contests but then grudgingly accepts their decision. Partly in deference to their authority, partly in recognition of past freedoms they have allowed, and partly in appreciation of their love for her, she gives in. The most persuasive factor to her, however, is *how* her parents conducted the disagreement—in a respectful, sensitive way.

Her parents listened to her point of view and took it seriously. They understood why attending was so important to her. They accepted how strong her feelings were, and they empathized with her disappointment at not being allowed to go. In consequence, she felt that she received a fair hearing. Equally important, she listened to her parents and understood why they said no. She understood the risks they foresaw, even though she did not agree that these concerns were fully justified. Now she and her parents know a little more about each other than they did before, and feel better known to each other. Their relationship feels stronger as a result. The resolution was not perfect since both sides have some regret: The parents regret they could not consent to what their daughter wanted, and she regrets what she will miss.

In this conflict, these parents kept their priorities straight. First, they sought *understanding*; second, they treated disagreement *nonjudgmentally*; third, they expressed *empathy*; and fourth, they worked for *resolution*. I believe this is the best way for parents to proceed in conflict with a child of any talking age. Instead of automatically tuning your child out, arguing with him, or ordering him to stop talking, *treat conflict with your child as a chance to communicate. Draw her out* with questions. "Can you tell me more?" "Can you help me better understand?" Instead of criticizing, *show appreciation for opposing opinions.* "You and I really see this issue differently." Now you have a basis to *empathetically connect* with the child and express sincere concern. "Can you tell me how all of this makes you feel?" And finally, *start the process of resolution.* "Let's see what we can work out."

When parents believe the primary objective in conflict with their child is to win their way, then they have already lost. They have lost the opportunity for communication that a difference in wants, values, or perceptions has created. Disagreements between parent and child do not mean there is something they can't talk about. It means that there is something they *need* to talk about. There is much at stake.

The child is an adult in training, learning from his parents relationship skills (such as how to conduct conflict) that he will take with him into adulthood. If he learns as a child to win disagreements by any means or to avoid them at all costs, this is how he is likely to treat conflict with a partner, and perhaps his children, when he is older.

Parents must be mindful that conflict is not something they *have* with their child; it is something they *do* with their child. *Conflict is a performance act.* Every time they engage in conflict with their child, they are *teaching* him by example and interaction how to manage conflict. Habits become established through repetition. So on each occasion of conflict, parents must model behavior that they want their child to learn. A parent who verbally threatens, emotionally bullies, or physically forces a young child into submission may win the battle, but the *means* severely compromise the *end*—the well-being of the relationship. A parent who uses intimidation and coercion loses some loving standing and trust in the child's eyes. Perhaps the parent has also unwittingly taught the child some tactics that will later be used by the teenager against the adult.

The family of origin is a training ground in conflict for parents. If you grew up in a family where disagreements were openly discussed and constructively resolved, then you will likely bring that approach into the family you create. Coming from this family background, you might say to a child: "There is no disagreement between us that I do not want to listen to and try to work out, even though it may not always be to your satisfaction." However, if you grew up in a home where conflict was not allowed or was actually unsafe, you may be at risk of either engaging in that behavior with your own children or avoiding conflict out of fear of receiving or inflicting harm. Coming from this family background, you might say to a child: "I don't want to discuss it!"

The degree to which parents are prepared to constructively manage conflict varies widely. On a continuum, there are parents at one extreme who are always up for a good debate, while at the opposite extreme there are parents who try to avoid all argument. You need to know where on this continuum *you* are because it will affect how you engage, or disengage, in conflict with your partner or children. Do not blame yourself if you become defensive or despotic during an argument with your child. By example, experience, or other instruction, you were probably taught to act that way, so treat this behavior as a chance to become more self-aware. Since parental conduct in conflict is always a matter of choice, it is always susceptible to being changed, if that is what you decide to do.

Regardless of their family background, it is helpful for all parents to understand that the focus of conflict tends to change when children enter adolescence. In their landmark study, *Relationship Conflict,* psychologists Daniel Canary, William Cupach, and Susan Messman observed that research about conflict in parent/child relationships "reflects two different conflict activities: one involving the young child trying to master his or her social world and one featuring the adolescent trying to understand changes due to puberty while asserting him- or herself as an individual."[1] I agree.

In my counseling work with families, I have found that parent/child conflict tends to be over issues of control and competence; parent/adolescent conflict tends to be about individuality and independence, two issues that often make disagreements more frequent and challenging during the teenage years. Adolescents often seem to thrive on arguments that seem pointless to parents. The truth is that most teenagers are eager and better equipped to take their parents on than are younger children. Why?

A younger child typically wants to have a lot in common with his or her parents, is willing to live on their terms, and takes pleasure in pleasing them. In adolescence, the teenager typically claims more commonality with peers and less with parents and pushes for more separation and differentiation at home, casting parents in an obstructionist role. This is why it behooves parents to start training the child early in talking and working out disagreements so that, come adolescence, they and the teenager are experienced at constructively coping with conflicts that will normally increase between them.

Stop the Screaming aims to help parents prepare themselves and their children to better manage conflict. Like any complex human behavior, conflict is *multiply determined,* meaning that in any given conflict a number of motivating factors are usually at play. Thus a tussle between young children sharing a toy can be the result of a disagreement over whose turn it should be, a competition for dominance, or of a need to ventilate frustration after a hard day at school. For simplicity's sake, however, I have separated out eight factors that can are involved in normal discord between parent and child or between siblings. They are cooperation, emotion, communication, intolerance, resemblance, change, authority, and compromise. These eight factors are closely related and often overlap, but a single chapter is devoted to each. For example, Chapter Five, "Resemblance and Conflict," includes an examination of sibling rivalry, although additional aspects of sibling conflict are discussed in other chapters as well. In general, I don't raise a problem about conflict without suggesting some resolution to it.

Within each chapter I include examples involving both children and adolescents so that parents with children of any age can relate the factor under discussion to their own family experience. However, since adolescence (roughly, age nine into the early- to mid-twenties) lasts significantly longer than childhood (roughly, birth to age eight or nine), and since adolescent conflict tends to be more frequent and intense, I include a few more examples from these challenging years. If you are a parent with young children, I hope that the adolescent examples will help to prepare you for the conflict-ridden teenage years ahead. And if you are a parent with adolescents, I hope that the childhood examples will help you understand how these factors have shaped your approach to conflict and how you may want to change your approach in the future. I close each chapter with three core ideas about conflict that you may want to carry away for further thought.

This book draws on my experience over twenty years as a psychologist in private counseling practice working primarily with white, middle-income, urban American families to help resolve troublesome conflicts to positive effect. Obviously, everything I have to say in this book is both informed and limited by my personal, social, and cultural background. Therefore, do not expect these ideas to be universally applicable. Rather, take those that seem to fit your circumstances and experience.

Finally, this is *not* a book about how to fight in order to win; it is a book about how to better understand and constructively conduct a wide variety of common parent/child conflicts, the occurrence of which will never go away. As one psychologist has noted, we tend to give conflict a bad name: "Conflict is almost universally perceived as a negative occurrence, a blemish on what most people expect should be a smooth and well-ordered life."[2] My hope is that *Stop the Screaming* will encourage parents to embrace conflict and treat it as an opportunity to communicate with their children, who will consequently learn to treat conflict in the same positive way.

1

COOPERATION AND CONFLICT

Conflict depends on the principle of cooperation: For the creation, conduct, and resolution of all family conflicts (between parents, parent and child, siblings) the participation of opposing parties is required. By accepting individual responsibility for their share in this cooperation, parents and children can influence the process and outcome of what occurs. If they cast off that responsibility by blaming each other, however, an amicable resolution will likely be impossible to reach.

HOW CONFLICT BEGINS

Think of it this way. Despite appearances to the contrary, no human conflict ever really starts between people: It starts *within* people. Each person makes a *judgment* that some issue is worth contesting and then decides to *engage* the other party in a response. The younger sister says to herself, "I don't like it that my brother hit me, and I'm going to hit him back."

Or consider the angry parent who is determined to "make" a silent child reveal what is bothering her because not knowing is bothering him. "If you don't tell me what's going on, you are going to bed early!" But angry demands only yield a more sullen response from the child.

It is better for the parent to explain that when she won't say what is upsetting her, it leaves him wondering what is amiss. He can only guess what the matter is, will probably guess wrong, and perhaps act on that misunderstanding in ways she won't like. "How can I help you feel better if you won't tell me what's wrong? I bet it's that you got into more trouble with the teacher today. I'm going to call her tonight." Now the child blurts out that her friend was mean to her on the playground today. The parent who was prepared for conflict because he felt shut out can now offer comfort instead.

What a person is *thinking* in the moment is the primary influence on whether she decides to initiate or collaborate in conflict. An eighteen-year-old once told me about a fight he almost started before he realized, just in time, that if he did, he would have major cause to regret it. "I'm driving down the highway when this pickup truck passes me and then swerves back in front of me so close I have to slam on the breaks to avoid rear-ending him. No way! Immediately, I'm tailgating this guy, cussing him out and furiously honking my horn. Finally, he gets off at an exit and pulls to a stop, with me right behind him. I jump out of my car, ready to get into it, when these two big guys get out of the truck, looking about as angry as I feel. That's when I say to myself, 'What am I thinking?' Then I turn around, get back in my car, and drive off." "What *were* you thinking?" I asked. "I was thinking, 'They shouldn't have cut me off! They shouldn't run me off the road that way! They can't get away with that! I'll make them sorry!'" In his mind, he had set up four conditions that made him determined to fight. Mental sets have action consequences this way. How one thinks affects what one does, as the young man fortunately realized at the last minute, taking responsibility for the conflict that started within him and could have escalated into a fight with strangers.

There is a lesson here. *If you have a young child who continually gets into fights on the playground, take time to find out what he is thinking before he fights.* Instead of punishing him for fighting, show him how he can choose to react in a way that does not automatically direct him into youthful combat. You might say, "When someone hurts your feelings, you think that you must hurt the person back. That's one way to react, but there are others. Let's talk about what those might be. You could let the person know you feel hurt and you could talk about it, or you might decide he didn't mean to hurt your feelings and let it go." Another level of thought involved in conflict is deciding whether engaging in it is worthwhile. If one party decides that it is not worthwhile or thinks that it is but the risks of engagement are too great, the internal requirements for conflict will not be met. The younger brother who is upset that his surly older sister has once again deliberately been mean to him decides the better part of wisdom is not to retaliate. Why give his sister the fight he knows she is spoiling for?

People are geared differently for conflict. Some people, child and adult, love to pick fights for the love of the contest. Then there are those who see little value in it, who can ignore the goading, mostly judging it not worth the energy to argue. *Readiness for conflict is a matter of internal choice*, which can often be the result of conflicts within oneself. For example, a child who feels unhappy over not standing up to his tormenters at school and wishes he had defended himself instead may pick a fight with a younger sibling at home later to act out his hurt, angry feelings.

Another example of the way internal conflict begets external conflict is teenage rebelliousness. Many parents misunderstand this, treating rebellious behavior as opposition directed against them personally, when it is not. The adolescent is actually in conflict with the compliant child she used to be and acts out against her parents in order to redefine herself on more independent terms. She wants to change herself and does so by challenging their authority. Teenage rebellious behavior is also a good example of how conflict can only begin when someone decides to lodge a complaint. A teenager's decision to object to something her parents are doing is only one of a series of choices required for an active conflict to unfold.

REQUIREMENTS FOR CONFLICT

It is important to understand that *conflict isn't just one choice*, but the culmination of a series of choices, with each step in the sequence a point at which a different choice could be made. Here are some stages of the parent/child conflict.

- Parent and child have a *difference* in conduct, habits, wants, values, beliefs, or perceptions that is brought into focus between them. For example, the child likes his room messy, which is *different* from how the parent likes it.
- Someone decides to lodge a *complaint*. The parent complains about her son's messy room and tells him to clean it up.
- The other party disputes or rejects this complaint, creating a *disagreement*. The son protests that his room isn't messy, it's comfortable.
- Both parties agree to *contest the disagreement*, creating a conflict. The parent insists that her son clean up his room. The child insists that he shouldn't have to.
- The conflict continues until a *resolution* is reached. The child agrees to clean up his room in an hour, after his TV show is over, and the parent agrees to delay satisfaction until this later time.

Some parents acknowledge differences and do not allow them to turn into active disagreements. They may think it is more important for their sixth-grader to get good grades than to have a lot of friends, while she has a reverse priority. They, wisely, don't waste time arguing over the relative importance of grades versus friends; they simply supervise their daughter to make sure she does her homework. Alternatively, active disagreements can remain unresolved, creating ongoing tension. Stepparent and stepchild, for example, may not be able to make lasting peace over the scope of the new adult's authority. Attempts at resolution do not last long; the differences soon arise again and arguing ensues. Siblings who managed to agree about who got to go first yesterday are back to fighting over the same issue today.

We all learn to live with and work around many more human differences than we use conflict to work through and resolve. We ignore, avoid, accept, and accommodate a host of unwelcome and offensive behaviors that we do not contest because we decide that the effort and emotional wear and tear it would take is not worthwhile. Family members are *selective* when it comes to engaging in conflict, choosing to create disagreements over only those differences they are not willing to live with. *It takes willingness to cooperate in conflict.*

HOW CONFLICT IS COOPERATIVE

The most important thing for parents to understand about conflict is that, although it is always about disagreement, it is fundamentally based on an agreement between a parent and child. When people argue, they actively agree to oppose each other's views, with the objective of convincing the other person to change his mind or behavior.

In counseling, when frustrated parents complain that they are trapped in endless conflict with their willful child, I suggest that they consider an alternative point of view: Conflict is collaborative and cooperative, *a joint undertaking* that requires teamwork. Parent and child work *together* to contest their differences. Your child can't have a fight with you unless you agree to fight back.

- It takes cooperation to start a conflict.
- It takes cooperation to maintain a conflict.
- And it takes cooperation to resolve a conflict.

The cooperative formula is this: *resistance vs. resistance = conflict.* Conflict arises from one resistance pushing against another resistance, and lasts only as long as both parties continue to invest energy in this mutual opposition. If one party gives up their resistance, the conflict ends. The weary father who ceases to debate with a maddening early adolescent, by simply announcing, "I have explained myself as much as I can and have nothing further to discuss, although I will listen to anything you have to say," liberates himself from the young person's untiring interest at this quarrelsome age in provoking argument for its own sake. The father will listen, but will not argue further.

In declining to argue back, however, the father is also giving something up. Withdrawing from conflict with an argumentative teenager is always a trade-off—the father gains relief from ongoing conflict but loses a valuable opportunity to learn more about his son. While arguing with a teenager is aggravating, it can also be informative. That is, it is better to treat a child, and particularly an adolescent, not as an opponent, but as an *informant,* whose different agenda and point of view open a window of understanding. Think of your child not as your enemy, but as a *partner* in disagreement, with whom you share a joint interest in working something out for the sake of the relationship. The parent can say, "Please tell me more about what you want and why, so I can better understand." Instead of shutting the child down, he uses conflict to draw her out. Now cooperation of an educational kind can begin.

If your child's resistance intensifies during an argument, it is usually best to disengage from debate at this pressure point. Delay pursuing the issue until the child has cooled down a bit. Then patiently, but persistently, bring up the subject again. Whenever practical, it's better for the parent to follow the *path of least resistance.* A power struggle with your child can quickly escalate, with damaging results. If your willful child is red in the face with angry determination to oppose you, acknowledge her frustration, and then disengage, with a promise to revisit the issue later. In the meantime, you can suggest doing something together, making a snack or watching TV to allow tempers to cool. "Later" is the tactic parents need to use when conflict with their child "now" is escalating. Resorting to "later" is not giving up or giving in. It is judiciously using delay so conflict can be resumed on less intense, more reasonable terms. To quote that anonymous aphorism about a parent's need for maturity, do not argue with a child when there is no thinking person at home.

WHEN SIBLINGS FIGHT

In a conflict between children, parents can fall into the trap of trying to fix responsibility. "Okay, who started it?" is a common refrain of parents called to the scene of battle. In trying to determine just who provoked whom in order to sanction the instigator, parents run the risk of ignoring the children's shared responsibility. When their kindergarten-age daughter runs in from the other room crying that her twelve-year-old brother has just pushed her, it is common to feel angry that the older, bigger child is picking on the younger, smaller one. Demanding to know whether what the little girl said is true, the parents are prepared to punish their son for bullying. "Yes," he angrily admits. Now they have him dead to rights. Or do they?

"But it was her fault," he protests, "not that you'd ever believe me!"

"A five-year-old starting a fight with a twelve-year-old?" they ask in predictable disbelief, "Come on!"

"See? You never want to hear my side!" he complains.

"Okay then, let's hear it," they say.

"I'm on the phone with my new girlfriend, and the little snoop walks right up next to me to listen in. I whispered for her to get away, but she refused to move, and then she said had the right to stand anywhere she wants. Then, with my hand over the receiver I asked her again to get away, but she just refused. That's when I gave her a push."

"Is this true?" the parents ask their daughter, who sullenly admits that it is.

Since the parents have agreed to listen, they can see that each child was at fault, and they can decide to hold both accountable. The little girl's provocation was a bid to engage her brother in conflict (perhaps to get his attention and then get him in trouble).

But no child can start a fight alone. The big brother's resistance signified his acceptance of her invitation to engage in conflict. The conflict ended when parents, as they so often do, intervened to shut both resistances down. "You are not to bother your brother when he is on the phone." "You are not to push your sister."

Sometimes parents will resolve their own conflicts by ceasing to contest a disagreement between them: They simply agree to let it go. A mother and father finally give up trying to change each other's mind about the importance of their child wearing clean clothes when visiting friends, deciding to let their disagreement over the child's public appearance stand. They reach a mutually acceptable solution by agreeing to let the parent who arranges the visit make the call. Now they have pulled one source of conflict off the table. The same strategy goes for children, too, when, for example, young siblings stop fighting over what TV show to watch and agree that they will each get to choose on alternate days.

There is just one caveat. Agreements can't be coerced. The parent says to the child, "You broke our agreement about not watching TV until homework is done." The child replies, "No I didn't. I broke *your* agreement. It was never mine. When you tell me I have to agree to something, that's not an agreement, that's a rule!" Score one for the child. For an agreement to be an agreement, the willing 'signatures' of both parties are required.

Choosing to engage in conflict is always an act of cooperation between two parties. What we *cannot* choose, however, is to live in a family without any conflict. As researchers in the field of conflict have noted, "The potential for conflict resides in the very activity of two people relating to each other."[1]

The antiwar bumper sticker had it right: "Suppose they gave a war and nobody came?" Or only one side came? War is a willing partnership of a very complex, destructive order. Conflict between parent and child is also a willing partnership. It is a *dance of disagreement* whose steps become harder to unlearn the more often they are practiced. Without our realizing it, conflict can become second nature. As one doctor describes it, "[F]amilies stuck in cycles of conflict find it very hard to change because old ways have become habits and unpleasant scenes are replayed over and over."[2]

RITUAL CONFLICTS

Ritual conflicts are fights that parent and child get into so routinely that they lose sight of the steps leading up to them. Consider the nightly homework debate recounted in counseling by a single parent and child. Three or four nights a week, it unfolds in the same way.

The players arrive on the home stage at about the same hour—the child from his after-school activity, the mother from work; both are tired and grumpy after their long days. The steps to nightly argument swiftly proceed as follows:

> *Parent*: "Please start your homework." (Request)
> *Child*: "I'll do it later." (Delay)
> *Parent*: "Do it now and get it over with." (Demand)
> *Child*: "Why should I have to do it now? I just got home. I'm tired."
>   (Challenge)
> *Parent*: "Because I'm tired too, and I said so." (Overrule)
> *Child*: "That's not fair! I won't!" (Refuse)
> *Parent*: "If you don't get started now, no TV later!" (Threaten)
> *Child*: "You can't make me!" (Defy)
> *Parent*: "You never do as I ask!" (Charge)
> *Child*: "You're always bossing me around!" (Countercharge)

In just seconds, they have laid the groundwork for their ritual argument again, parent and twelve-year-old both believing that it is the other person's fault.

> *Parent*: "Well, if you would just do as I ask when I ask, we wouldn't
>   have to argue."
> *Child*: "Well, if you would just let me get on the computer after school,
>   we wouldn't *be* arguing."
> *Parent*: "When I do, the later you wait, the longer homework takes."
> *Child*: "When you don't, the harder it is to get homework done."

As you can see, each party chooses to enter the ritual conflict, airing their entire repertory of bottled-up grievances. At each step, parent and child each could have made a different choice and forestalled the conflict. The parent could have greeted the child with concern about his long day, instead of immediately telling him to do his homework. The child could have started his homework instead of pushing for a delay. The mother could have empathized with his fatigue and allowed him a half hour on the computer instead of escalating the request into a demand. The child could have negotiated a deal: "I'll start it now and finish the rest after dinner." Any one of these acknowledgements of what the other wanted could have ended their resistance.

So if they have other options, why do the boy and his mother do the same dance of disagreement night after night? Partly because it is familiar, a predictable, well-worn interaction that doesn't require much thinking at the end of the long day. Conflict has become their greeting ritual. Oddly enough, it connects them. They make contact, exchange a few irritated words, and relieve a little accumulated tension.

"And then what?" I say to the child. "After you stop arguing, what happens?"

"Oh," the child shrugs, "after the fight is over, I do what I was told."

"You mean you end up doing what your Mom wanted when you could have acted differently to begin with and avoided all the aggravation?" I ask.

"Well," he replies, "my Mom had different choices too!" And I agree.

To end a ritual conflict, you have to recognize that you are getting something out of the confrontation. Maybe you are both tired and irritable and need an outlet for blowing off some steam. If so, consider saying something like this to your child. "We've been in this hard place many times before and it hasn't worked out well for either of us. We just end up feeling frustrated, raising our voices, and getting mad. So, let's take a timeout before it gets too late. Let's separate for an agreed upon time, both cool down, and each try to think of other choices we could make. Then let's get back together and *start over*, to see if we can work our needs out in a better way." *Whenever you find yourself caught up in a ritual conflict, stop action, separate for an agreed upon time to think, then restart the disagreement prepared to try to communicate in a different way.* Conflict is like a dance of collaborative steps that each partner can always choose to change, thereby encouraging the other person to do the same.

Ritual conflicts also illustrate another principle of conflict: the principle of *attraction*. Conflict occurs when both principles are in play—attraction to confront a difference and cooperation to contest it.

THE PRINCIPLE OF
ATTRACTION IN CONFLICT

Parent and child, or rival siblings, are drawn toward disagreement because *opposites attract*. Contrast is defined, cause for debate is raised, grounds for a contest are established, and the opportunity for active competition is created. Both parties can be enticed by the opportunity to confront each other over their differences in order to engage in opposition. For example, two young children sharing the back seat of the car may draw an invisible dividing line down the middle of the seat to alleviate their boredom. They have artfully created a difference— "my side" versus "your side"—that immediately gets their attention as each one challenges the other to stay on his side of the line. In fact, one good thing about conflict is that while it is happening, neither party is left unoccupied, which suggests that, like these two children, people sometimes create conflict when they are feeling bored.

Boredom is not the neutral state that most parents tend to believe it to be. It is actually a state of loneliness in which the child feels unable to connect to himself, to other people, or to his surroundings in a meaningful way. It is a state of disconnection that is isolating and anxiety provoking. Conflict relieves the loneliness of boredom by forging an oppositional connection that may not be happy, but beats the misery of feeling alone. This is how boredom can be a staging area for conflict.

Once the attraction of opposites is in place, the children have a chance to do something with each other so neither has to feel at a loose end, disconnected, lonely, and bored. Now they have something to fight about. The decision to cooperate and contest the difference, in this case the imaginary dividing line, is what it takes to consummate the conflict. The two children poke and provoke each other to defend their space or fight over exactly where that line should be placed. If their parents wonder how they can fight over a dividing line that neither can see, they are failing to appreciate that conflict is a form of connection. By engaging with one another in conflict, the children create companionship with each other. It's like adult partners who bicker all the time. They are attracted by the irritations between them, and their conflict keeps them married in disagreement; an unhappy connection feels better than none at all.

If you ever find yourself in a heated argument with your adolescent over an issue that doesn't seem to justify the magnitude of the conflict, ask yourself, "Is my teenager just feeling bored or lonely?" If you think he is, try interrupting the fight to say something like, "I don't know about you, but I'm feeling really tired and would enjoy doing something fun together, maybe watching a movie or getting something to eat. Afterwards, we can get back to our disagreement if you like." Sharing an enjoyable activity satisfies your teenager's need to feel connected with you, and the invitation to renew the conflict is usually not accepted.

During her adolescence, conflict can be an ideal medium for your teenager to stay in contact with you—fighting both brings you together and creates distance between you. In the process, she gets to

- define a difference between you,
- communicate with you,
- challenge your authority,
- declare independence,
- demand respect,
- hold your attention,
- ventilate frustration,
- create an intense connection,
- and, finally, feel separate from you.

The challenge for parents is to find *alternative* ways for their teenagers to stay adequately connected to them during their lonely journey toward personal and social autonomy. Both disengaging and engaging in conflict can be difficult.

CONFLICT CAN BE CHALLENGING TO DO

Parenting a teenager is neither a popularity contest nor a peaceful undertaking. As you advocate behavior that you feel is in your teenager's best interests, you run up against a young person who strenuously objects to your decisions. This will happen when you dare to

- ask about what he doesn't want to discuss,
- confront him on behavior he wants ignored,
- demand effort he doesn't want to make,
- deny the freedom he requests,
- insist on agreements he doesn't want to keep,
- hold him accountable for consequences he doesn't want to face,
- or correct him for misbehavior.

He will not thank you for acting responsibly. Instead, he will complain, criticize, and argue. In general, such encounters are much more wearing on you than on him. Your teenager can actually feel energized as he asserts his independence. The same cannot usually be said for parents, who may just want to rest and recuperate after a conflict with their adolescent, while the teenager happily talks on the phone to a friend, as if nothing has happened. The parent is like an amateur boxer who is exhausted after going a few rounds against a seasoned professional who is not even winded by the exercise.

Conflict with a younger child can also require parental endurance, particularly if the child is strong willed and determined to challenge you over issues of control. Although you might need to engage in conflict over important rules—for example, that your four-year-old always hold your hand when crossing the street—you must be selective about cooperating in lesser disagreements. The adult energy it takes to argue over whether your second-grader can wear mismatched socks to school may just not be worth it.

AVOIDING CONFLICT

During a child's early adolescence (ages nine to thirteen), parents need to have good *conflict avoidance* skills because the child will be testing her powers of persuasion and pushing boundaries. You need to know how *not* to automatically accept every invitation to engage in another dispute. With children at this age, a parent needs to explain and insist, but not defend and rebut. One adult remembered a phrase her farmer father used to limit debate when she was a teenager: "I don't want to hear your philosophy if it doesn't grow corn."[3] He meant that he was not willing to waste energy in arguing over what did not truly matter.

Sometimes a young child will up the ante in his bid for a conflict with parents, throwing down an *outrageous challenge* too tempting to refuse, and when a parent picks it up, the fight begins. What the child wants to do is to keep the issue in play at all costs in the hopes that he will wear you down. But he can't bring you back into the conflict if you decline to argue any further. Threats of extreme action and dire consequences are one ploy a child uses to reengage parents who have said their final word about a lesser disagreement.

The child says: "If we can't talk any more about this...

- "I'll stop going to school!"
- "I'll make myself sick!"
- "I'll run away!"

The best approach is to avoid conflict over these issues. *Leave the challenge on the table.* Instead, say, "Those don't sound like very happy decisions for you to make and we'd be sorry if you made them. But our decision about your not going over to a friend's house on a school night is firm."

Parents should *not* avoid conflict when

- confusion or misunderstanding stemming from a disagreement may worsen;
- you feel intimidated by your child's anger, thereby giving her emotionally extortionate power;
- your inconsistency in enforcing rules undermines the child's willingness to comply;
- false interpretations and assumptions start distorting what the conflict is actually about;
- you store up hurt or resentment because you didn't speak up;
- you create a habit of avoidance that makes it harder to confront the child the next time around;

- it means that you let unacceptable behavior go unchallenged. Your words or actions communicate: "I would rather put up with what I don't like than fight about it."

Do not cooperate with more conflict than you have energy for; but do not avoid conflict when the immediate relief is outweighed by a larger or long-term cost. Parents who are conflict averse with a child when he or she is growing up, avoiding disagreements out of discomfort, refusing to stick to stands or limits when the child argues back, can pay a very painful price for that history of avoidance when the child is grown. Then, even though love may still be strong, there can be an irrecoverable loss of respect for parents who lacked the courage and commitment to fight with the child for the child's best interests against what he or she wanted at the time.

As for that common rationale for avoiding conflict, "I didn't want to hurt your feelings," this is self-protection in disguise. "I didn't say anything because if you got upset, I would end up feeling bad." But be aware of the "conflict fatigue" that comes from cooperating in conflict too much.

CONFLICT FATIGUE

Because fatigue tends to diminish perspective, feeling "tired of fighting" can make it hard for parents to see their cooperative role in the conflict. When you are worn down by recurrent conflict with a strong-willed child, for example, you may focus on your child's behavior, blaming the conflict on him, unwittingly diminishing your own capacity to influence the outcome of what is going on. *The most common mistake made by parents who have more conflict with their child than they want is ignoring their own collusion in the process.* Whenever you find yourself in a recurring conflict with your child, identify your own involvement by asking yourself these *complicity* questions:

- "Why am I choosing to cooperate in this conflict?" Are you in this conflict for a good reason or are you just being emotionally reactive?

- "Is this conflict worthwhile?" Are you likely to win your point, support your stand, defend your interests, or get your way?
- "Am I modeling a way of dealing with conflict I want my child to emulate?" Are you communicating a tone and language that you would want your child to use with you?
- "What am I doing or not doing that is sustaining the conflict or making it worse?" Are your positions or tactics counterproductive to what you want out of the conflict?
- "What can I do differently that might lead to a favorable outcome?" What words could you say or what actions could you take that might encourage the resolution you would like?

When you accept your share of cooperative responsibility in a conflict, you retain influence over the outcome by claiming your choices.

For example, many parents have difficulty getting a small child to go to bed, stay in bed, and sleep in her own bed. By the time they come to counseling for help, they are weary, discouraged, and angry with the child for turning bedtime into battle every night. Then they tell me everything the child is doing to cause the problem. This is when I shift the focus to their role in the conflict by asking the complicity questions.

- Why are you cooperating in the conflict? "To get her to bed on time and stay there."
- Is the conflict worthwhile? "Yes, because until we get her down we can't get the rest we need."
- Are you modeling in conflict the kind of conduct you want your child to emulate? "No, because the more upset we act the more upset she acts."
- What are you doing or not doing that may be making things worse? "We are acting angry, and the angrier we act, the more she begs and clings and cries. The guiltier we feel, the more we let her stay up a little later to feel better. Then, of course, she still resists going down."
- What could you do differently that might lead to favorable outcome "We could act loving and firm, instead of angry and inconsistent."

The bedtime conflict is successfully resolved when parents learn to empathize with their child's feelings. They explain their need for this bedtime arrangement, and let her know that if she needs to cry about her sadness with their decision, that is okay. And if she keeps getting up and coming out, with a kiss and an "I love you," they patiently put the child back in bed without further attention for as many nights as it takes, until she finally gives up her resistance and accepts going to bed on their terms. By assuming responsibility for their role in the conflict and then consistently communicating caring and determination, they finally persuade the child to give the contest up.

In conflict with a child, parental vision often tends to become *monocular*. They see only the child's opposition. What they need to maintain is *binocular* vision—the capacity to see their own behavior *and* how it interacts with the child's. As one writer succinctly puts it, taking responsibility for "our own behavior leads the way to family change."[4]

It is when parents cannot do this that disagreements grow intractable and the lines of opposition become more stubbornly drawn. As long as they continue responding the same way, the child is not likely to change her behavior. The old saw rings true: "If all you ever do is all you've ever done, then all you'll ever get is all you've ever got." Or as Albert Einstein put it, "the definition of insanity is continuing to try the same approach to solve a problem but expecting different results."[5] *When you have a "bedtime problem" with your child, you must change your behavior to help the child change hers.*

ROADBLOCKS TO RESPONSIBILITY: BLAME AND PRIDE

Two things typically indicate that someone is not accepting responsibility in conflict: blame and pride. In addition to intensifying emotions, blame places all the responsibility on the other person. The blamer assumes the victim role. After all, if the conflict is the other person's doing, the blamer has little power to influence the outcome. As I heard one older sister tell her frustrated parents about her constant fighting with her younger sister: "Well if it's all my fault, then she's got no good way to help stop it!"

Blamers often feel that if they criticize an opponent enough, the other person will change his behavior. This rarely works. Instead, *blame empowers the opposition.* The blame equation is *conflict = (all) you.* The responsibility equation is *conflict = (partly) you + (partly) me.* And blame *exaggerates* its claims.

Because blame often traffics in absolutes—the accusations "You never do..."/"You always say..."—it allows no middle ground. *Sometimes* you do, *sometimes* you don't. Yet, there is often a seed of truth in an accusation that the other person can accept. "Mostly I don't think I do what you say, but I guess sometimes I do, and I will try to be better about that." Such acceptance of responsibility can open a dialogue instead of a fight. The parent says to the sullen teenager: "I think we are getting nowhere in this discussion, and you are right, it's partly my fault. What I would like to do is start this conversation over a different way. Could you please help me understand what I am missing in what is going on, and how you feel? That is where I would like to begin." In conflict, it is usually better to end than to begin the argument with blame. Begin with blame, and accusation encourages defensiveness that antagonizes the discussion. Postpone blame until the end, when the disagreement has been sorted out, and blame becomes the mutually agreed upon allocation of responsibility.

When both parent and child assume the mantle of the "injured party," preferring to feel wronged than to admit complicity, blame creates standoffs. This is where pride enters the fray. Both parent and child remain committed to being "right," stubbornly telling themselves,

- I won't back down, give in, be beaten.
- I will win, save face, have the last word.
- I won't give to you until I get from you first.
- I will stay as I am until you change toward me.

Such proud, willful parents and children can't bear to lose an argument or to simply let an argument go. As one psychologist observed, "[T]here are some people who seem to thrive on keeping a conflict going."[6] Parents who insist they are right can be relentless in an argument. "Don't you know," asks the exasperated child, "that not everyone believes like you?" "Of course I do," snaps the parent. "But I also know they should!"

There is no arguing with pride. People who listen with their minds made up do not really listen at all. The only way out of an argument with such a person is to decide to let the difference between you stand. *When winning becomes more important to one party than understanding, then conflict ceases to generate useful information.*

Pride refuses to relent on principle. Pride is often more of a roadblock for fathers because men tend to view disagreement as a performance issue. Conflict is a competition, and they feel they must win because their self-esteem is at stake. In contrast, women are often more prone to treat conflict as a communication issue, a chance to create understanding, because for them the welfare of the relationship is at stake. In counseling, I have frequently seen conflict between a father and a son in his late teens founder when each "man" refuses to back down. The dad won't help financially with college unless the son achieves higher grades in high school, while the son refuses to perform up to his father's terms and declares that after graduation he will make it on his own. Unbending pride keeps each man stuck in the stand he has stubbornly taken.

In such standoff situations, I typically ask them both: "If things continue this way, with no resolution to your disputes, what will happen to your relationship?" The answer usually is, "It will get worse." Then I tell them, "You each have to create an incentive for change. When you are stuck in opposition like this, what do you miss doing together?" In response, both agree that one important thing they miss is going to sports events together and sharing that enjoyment. When they are this mad at each other, they have to give that up. "That seems sad," I say. "It might be worthwhile to soften your stands over school with each other just enough to allow some of the good time together you miss." And that incentive enables them each to put some pride aside and work with the other to get what both value.

Not only does it take cooperation to prolong conflict, but also to create it.

COOPERATION CREATES CONFLICT

It is truly one of the most ignorant questions that parents, myself included, have asked siblings who are quarrelling over the use of a toy: "Why can't you just cooperate, why can't you learn to share?" Our question makes it sound like cooperation and sharing is easy, which is hardly the case. Cooperation requires working together; it also requires making joint decisions that meet some mutually acceptable standard of fairness, and disagreement must be managed, something that young children may not find easy to do. *Not only does conflict require cooperation; cooperation can create conflict.*

Suppose a parent assigns two children the job of cleaning the toy closet. Immediately, the kids are faced with a number of questions.

- Who is boss?
- Who gets to do what?
- Who gets to have what?
- Whose way is the right way?

When the fighting starts, the aggravated parent asks: "Why can't you get the job done without bickering with each other?" She could have limited conflict by answering the cooperation questions herself. "I am boss, I will decide who gets to do what, who gets to get what, and what is the right way." By claiming these decisions, she has diverted potential conflict away from them and toward herself, but having them argue with her rather than with each other is usually a more efficient way to get the job done.

Another approach is to mediate a settlement. If your son and daughter are arguing over who gets the last piece of cake, for example, you can propose a compromise, "One of you gets to cut it in half and the other gets to choose his piece first." For the "slicer," going first feels like a win, and he is motivated to keep the two halves "equal." The "chooser," who is no doubt microscopically attuned to any minute difference in the size of the "halves," feels like the winner when he gets the bigger piece.

UNFAIRNESS

Unfairness is a cooperation issue that arises when sharing feels inequitable. Children are always accusing parents of being unfair. A sister complains that a brother has freedom that is denied to her, that a chore is demanded from one sibling that another is spared, imposing a double standard that is unjust. Sometimes a child will even accuse parents of the worst kind of unfairness of all, *favoritism*, attributing inequitable treatment to the parents' greater preference for the other child: "She's your favorite!" is a charge that can be hard to hear. You don't want to admit to yourself that you might possibly appear to love one child less than another. But the accusation isn't really that you love the other child more; his grievance is that at this moment you are behaving in a way that is advantageous to his brother or sister. Rest assured that the complaint is not about love.

You might diffuse the feeling by saying something to show how silly it is. "You are right, she is our favorite—our favorite oldest child. And you are our favorite second child. And your brother is our favorite third child. You are all our favorites because each of you is the only one of you there is, and you are each unique and irreplaceable in our life."

The other thing to remember is that fairness always involves a double standard. Each child wants both special treatment and to be treated the same as her siblings. Thus your teenager daughter wants more freedom than her ten-year-old sister: "Since I'm more grown-up, it's only fair!" Yet when it comes to doing chores, she complains, "Why should I have to do more work than she does. It's not fair!" This places parents in a double bind. And that's not fair to them. Perhaps the best parents can do is strive to be equally unfair, as gauged by the numbers of complaints of *un*evenhandedness lodged against each of them. More to the point, when accused of unfairness, parents should explain, "Our job is not to treat you equally but appropriately, according to your individual needs." But we should remember that anonymous piece of wisdom: "Blessed be the mediator for he shall be hated by both sides." The compromise parents reach rarely gives either child 100% of what he or she wants. This is something about which both children can agree: "When you decide for us, you're always unfair!"

Unfairness can also be a divisive issue between marriage partners when they become parents. One of the most challenging tasks for new parents is to decide how to share childcare responsibilities. How will the couple redefine their relationship to incorporate the new baby? It is best to tackle this issue as soon as the first child is born in order to stave off these common complaints later on:

- "This relationship is all you!" The new father may feel he is being treated as a second-class citizen when it comes to making major baby care decisions. "You have taken control of everything that happens with our baby and I have no significant say at all!"
- "This relationship is all me!" The new mother may feel she has all the responsibility for making baby care decisions and that the father is bowing out. "I feel like I'm supposed to be in charge of all this new responsibility, and you won't do your part!"
- "This relationship is all us!" The new father may feel suffocated from lack of personal time now that he has become a parent. "I never have time for myself anymore!"
- "There is no us in the relationship!" New parents may feel that childcare responsibilities are pushing them apart. The new mother may complain, "You take care of the baby, and I take a rest. I take care of the baby, and you take a rest. We have no time together. I didn't have a baby to give up the marriage, but that's what it feels like has happened!"

Management of these issues will continue to be necessary until your children finally graduate your care. Here are three guidelines for how to make it work.

1. *Whatever sharing decision is made must be acceptable to both parents.* Mutually acceptable doesn't necessarily mean equal or ideal. It means compromise (reaching a middle ground where both get some

of what each wants) or concession (giving in on an issue of greater importance to the other person). Parents may not feel enthusiastic about all the sharing decisions they make, but they can be at peace with their decisions. Compromise becomes the primary rule of decision making when it comes to sharing because it is a losing and a winning proposition in one. Compromise is a losing proposition insofar as both parents get less than 100% of what they want. Compromise is a winning proposition, however, because each has sacrificed something for the good of the relationship, upon which the well-being of their marriage and of their child rearing depends.

2. *Whenever a previous sharing agreement becomes untenable, it needs to be thrown open for discussion and renegotiation.* A sharing decision that one partner pick up the child at daycare worked before she got a new job. Changing circumstances and needs mean that most arrangements won't work forever. Sickness or the demands of a new job can change the household. Sharing agreements must continually be adjusted. They last only as long as they continue to be acceptable to both parties. When a partner's ailing parent requires attention, the other partner has to pick up a greater share of childcare for a while. When one partner goes back to school part time to improve employability, the other partner may have more childcare to do.

3. *Listen to your partner when he or she is voicing any of the four common sharing complaints.* Ignoring these complaints allows bad feelings to grow between you. Disunity between parents makes children feel insecure. Pay particular attention to the complaint of unfairness, since that can generate so much resentment. And remember that just as children fight over sharing, so do adults.

Dispute over who is doing his or her *fair share* is another issue that parents may want to raise with a child they feel is making an *insufficient contribution* to the family. Frustrated parents complain, "All you ever think about is yourself! You act like this is a one-way, all your way, relationship! We keep giving and get no cooperation in return. What about giving something to us?" These complaints are especially common in early and mid-adolescence (ages nine to fifteen), and your teenager is usually guilty as charged. Weary of the resistance and arguing of early adolescence and the self-centeredness of mid-adolescence, parents feel unfairly treated because there is a lack of mutuality in the relationship. Parents are to some degree complicit in this situation if they have not taught the teenager in childhood to contribute to the family as a matter of course. Sometimes this happens because parents are overindulgent, but often it occurs out of the misplaced expectation that by doing for the child, she will learn from parental example to do for them. In fact, some children do seem to learn giving this way, but others simply learn to become takers. However, better late than never, so parents must now start holding the teenager accountable. They do so by doing nothing that the child asks, providing nothing that the child wants, without getting some meaningful act of cooperation and contribution from him first. So the parent says, "Sure, I'd be happy to drive you over to your friend's, but before I do, I need you to take out the garbage." To this condition, the teenager replies, "I will, I promise, after I get back. Can we go now?" But experience has taught the parent how such promises are false currency and that only performance counts. So he calmly and pleasantly insists, "After you do what I have asked, I will be happy to do what you want."

Parents should not waste time and energy complaining, arguing, or punishing a child to get a more cooperative exchange. The child is dependent on them for a host of services, resources, and permissions. To redress the imbalance of contribution and restore a sense of fairness with their child, they simply need to take a healthy stand and withhold what is requested or expected until they receive some act of cooperation first.

THREE IDEAS ABOUT
COOPERATION AND CONFLICT
TO CARRY FORWARD

- Conflict results from the willing collaboration of two parties, parent and child, to agree to disagree and mutually contest a point of difference between them.

- Conflict is a matter of mutual choice that requires the cooperation of parent and child for them to jointly confront, conduct, and resolve their disagreement.
- Cooperation creates conflict, between siblings for example, by raising questions over how to share a common interest and decide what constitutes a fair share.

2

EMOTION AND CONFLICT

Ever present in family conflict is the problematic role that emotion can play. To the good, emotion can sensitize parent and child to each other's feelings; to the bad, it can become too intense, inflaming feelings, impairing judgment, and reducing wiser self-restraint. Conflict with loved ones is no time to let your emotions determine what you say or do.

EMOTIONAL AROUSAL

In family conflicts, resolving the disagreement must always be secondary to the number one priority: safely managing the interaction. As researchers have noted, "one of the salient features of conflict is the arousal it generates."[1] When emotions rule, there is always a risk that physical or emotional damage will be done. Emotional arousal is the major threat to safety.

To say that emotions should not rule conflict by no means invalidates the importance of honoring feelings in conflict. It is important for a parent and child who are engaged in struggle to be emotionally sensitive not just to what each is thinking, but to what each is feeling as well. Thus the parent and the six-year-old who are late getting out of the house in the morning and blaming each other for the delay can relax some of the tension between them by taking less than a minute's extra time to show concern for each other's feelings. So the parent says, "I know you hate feeling rushed in the morning, and my getting impatient just makes those feelings worse. Tomorrow I will do a better job helping us get ready." And the child, feeling encouraged to take some responsibility for the situation replies, "I know you don't like feeling impatient, and tomorrow I will get going faster." In a conflict between parent and child, feelings are to be talked about, not acted on. In the heat of battle, emotion must be an informer, not a decider.

A corollary to this is the principle of *no carryovers.* If you or your child still feel anger over a past argument or anxiety over the next conflict, you need to talk about these feelings or your next disagreement will likely be more emotionally loaded. There is a distinction to be made here: *family conflict does not have to feel emotionally comfortable, but it must feel emotionally safe.*

A WORD ABOUT VIOLENCE: VERBAL (CRUELTY), EMOTIONAL (RAGE), PHYSICAL (BLOWS)

As researchers have noted, "People experience conflict in their most important, close relationships. How people manage their conflicts affects their ... risk of interpersonal violence."[2] I do not suppose that readers of this book are in danger of allowing family conflict to escalate to the point of injury, but I do believe that it is important to be aware that the danger is always there. The emotional intensity within families simply creates this unhappy possibility.

There are six scenarios that should be of concern:

- *When a family member repeatedly throws fits of temper or tantrums.* Living around unpredictable emotional explosiveness does not feel safe.
- *When a family member attacks objects or pets.* Living around someone who throws or breaks things or physically abuses a pet does not feel safe.

- *When a family member threatens to injure other family members (or herself).* Living around threats of personal harm does not feel safe.
- *When a family member deliberately injures himself or another family member.* Living around the harming of another family member does not feel safe.
- *When a family member verbally, emotionally, or physically abuses you.* Living with someone who batters you in any form does not feel safe.
- *When a family member repeatedly uses violence to force subservience, satisfy wants, and maintain control.* Living with someone who rules by intimidation does not feel safe.

In the family,

- conflict never justifies doing anyone harm,
- violence against one is threatening to all, and
- if injury does occur, it should be accidental, never intentional.

During an argument, emotions are good informants when alerting us to our feeling state, but bad advisors when impelling us to injure those we love. All parties to a conflict—child with sibling, parent with child, parent with parent—must take responsibility for managing their own emotional arousal. To do so requires recognizing a critical distinction—the difference between impulsive and deliberate decision making.

IMPULSIVE VERSUS DELIBERATE DECISION MAKING

Conflict should involve deliberate decision making, never the impulsive kind. *Impulsive decision making* is rash and relies on "thoughtless" functions—emotions, desires, and an urgent need to satisfy wants. Its frame of reference is the *present;* the focus is on instant gratification, what needs to happen *now.* Reactions are automatic and unquestioned and usually occur in a state of stimulation or arousal. *Deliberate decision making* is rational, restrained, and relies on "thoughtful" functions: perspective, analysis, and judgment. Its frame of reference reaches beyond the present and includes past experience and future possibilities. Reactions are measured and weighed. Gratification is delayed, allowing time for consideration, evaluation, or reflection.

As one psychologist points out, "Emotions are inborn, generated automatically in the most primitive, reptilian, limbic portion of our brain."[3] On the most primitive level, emotions are a direct expression of needs *in the moment.* The baby reaches for what she wants or cries at what she doesn't like. Impulsive decision making is driven more by force of feeling and urgency than by well-considered thought.

Deliberate decision making is rooted in another part of the brain. As another psychologist points out, "The prefrontal cortex seems to be at work when someone is fearful or enraged, but stifles or controls the feeling in order to deal more effectively with the situation at hand, or when a reappraisal calls for a completely different response.... The neo-cortical area of the brain brings a more analytic or appropriate response to our emotional impulses, modulating the amygdala and other limbic areas."[4] This capacity is "what scientists call 'executive function,' the set of abilities that allows you to select behavior that's appropriate to the situation, inhibit inappropriate behavior, and focus on the job at hand in spite of distractions."[5]

Both styles of decision making are valuable. Deliberateness is essential for monitoring, evaluating, preparing, and planning. Impulsiveness is at the heart of play, creativity, loving intimacy, and spontaneity. As one psychologist puts it, "[T]he complementarity of limbic system and neocortex...means each is a full partner in mental life...to harmonize head and heart."[6] In family conflict, however, deliberate decision making should be the leading partner. We need to teach our children how to slow decision making down by exercising self-restraint over impulse, instituting sufficient delay for time to think, considering what is wise before reacting. The lessons should start when they are very young. As one parenting expert writes, "[Y]our youngster may lack the self-control to express his anger peacefully. Instead, he may naturally lash out, perhaps hitting or biting in frustration. When this happens, he needs you to take control for him and to help him develop judgment, self-discipline, and other tools he needs in order to express his feelings in more acceptable and age-appropriate ways. . . . The best way to teach these lessons is to supervise your child carefully when he's involved in disputes. . . . Always watch your own behavior around your child. One of the best ways to teach him appropriate behavior is to control your own temper. If you express your anger in quiet, peaceful ways, he will probably follow your example."[7] You will have some re-teaching to do with the early- to mid-adolescent, when the hormonal influence of puberty can cause a *primal shift* back toward more emotional intensity and impulsive decision making. Model what you teach and your actions will instruct.

You can teach a very young child (age four and above) to control her impulsiveness by teaching her to ask herself the following five questions:

- What do I feel? ("I am feeling angry at you.")
- What do I think? ("I think you are unfair.")
- What do I want? ("I want to get back at you.")
- If I do what I want will I get what I want? ("No, we will just keep fighting.")
- What is wise? ("To talk about what happened and make peace.")

It takes practice to transition from impulsiveness to deliberation in conflict. It is a parent's job to help young children learn this skill, to regulate one's conduct in conflict by going at a *deliberate* speed.

LEARN TO APOLOGIZE

If, during an argument, you impulsively say or do something that hurts your child, it is important to apologize immediately. One psychologist asks parents, "Do you know how to apologize and make amends? Being human, we all make emotional mistakes and hurt others. But we must learn to recognize what we have done wrong and fix it. To do this, we have to take responsibility, ask for forgiveness, and make amends. This can involve changing our behavior if it hurts someone. These tasks aren't easy, but if we don't carry them out, our unacknowledged mistakes will permanently poison our relationships."[8] The steps you should model or take to undo such an injury are these:

- Take responsibility for what you have done. "In the heat of argument, I called you a loser." Apologize honestly for what you have done. "I am sorry that I called you a loser."
- Listen to your child talk about his injured feelings. "I want to hear about the hurt I have done."
- Offer to make amends where you meaningfully can. "I would like to do something that celebrates how well I think of you."
- And promise to never act in that hurtful way again. "I won't call you names again."

TEACHING CHILDREN TO APOLOGIZE

Suppose your ten-year-old son grabs the remote control from his six-year-old sister, who is crying because he switched her favorite TV show to his. When you tell him to give it back and let her watch her show, he throws the remote down and storms out of the room, but not before adding insult to injury: "Oh, let the baby have her bottle!"

Now he is angry and so are you. You want him to apologize and call after him, "And don't you come out of your room until you're ready to say you're sorry to your sister!"

You want him to express remorse for behaving badly, although you know a forced apology will not mean much. Oh, he's sorry all right, but not for making his sister cry.

- He is sorry he didn't get what he wanted.
- He is sorry that you reprimanded him and that he is in trouble with you.
- He is sorry to be on the losing end of the conflict with his little sister.

So how are you going to mend the relationship if any apology he makes will be insincere? The answer is simple: Don't go for an apology, go for an actual *mend*.

Let your son know that before he gets to do anything else that requires your permission, the mending must take place, and it must take place in conversation with *you*. It is a three-step process.

Step one is *sensitization*. You want him to be emotionally sensitive to how his behavior may have hurt his sister, so you pose a role reversal question. "Suppose you are six and your older brother grabs the remote and changes the channel to the show he wants to watch, and then calls you a hurtful name for acting upset. I want you to tell me three ways you might feel in that situation." The goal of sensitization is to create a sense of empathy.

Step two is *evaluation*. You want him to place his behavior in an ethical context, so you pose an examination question. "In your judgment, setting your anger aside, do you believe that the way you treated your sister is okay? If you believe it is okay, give me three reasons why. If you believe it was wrong, give me three reasons why. Then let's talk about it." The goal of evaluation is to create a moral framework for his actions.

Step three is *reparation*. You want to place his behavior in the context of injury given, so you pose a recovery question. "What special act of amends could you make to your sister?" The goal of reparation is atonement. If, as part of the amends, he wants to apologize, that is up to him. But it must be in addition to whatever act of atonement he makes.

Parents often prefer a forced apology to an actual mending because the mending process takes attention and effort that a token apology does not. I believe mending is worth the time it takes because it can teach a valuable lesson about how to recover normal caring after some hurt is given or received, as inevitably happens in all significant relationships. Remember that a child is just an adult in training, and as parents we are preparing that young person to manage later relationships. Do you want to send a young person out into the world without preparing him to manage the inevitable mistakes he will make in his significant attachments?

Parents who neglect this education are often those who expect apologies from others but are constitutionally incapable of making apologies themselves. I am referring here to those parents who can't admit to or make up for wronging others because they can't bear being in the wrong.

Parents who are best at teaching children how to mend relationships are those who accept responsibility for their behavior. They can admit that they hurt their child, offer a *meaningful apology,* expressing *authentic sorrow* for what they did, and take steps to repair whatever damage has been done. More important, they resolve never to act that way again and they *keep that resolution.* These are parents who are modeling mending.

But, going back to our example, what about the younger sister? What is her role in the mending process? A very important one: It's called *forgiveness.*

Suppose the angry and hurt little girl says to her mother: "I don't care what he does to make it up to me, I won't forgive him, ever!" Now the mom has some more work to do. She has to explain whom forgiveness primarily benefits. "It's not just for your brother, although it's partly to let him know that you are okay with him again. It is mostly for you, so you don't have to hold on to your feelings of hurt and anger. People who can't forgive carry resentment around inside of them. Forgiveness lets you let it go. When people make an honest effort to make up for what they did, our job is to forgive them so we can get back to keeping each other good company."

SETTING AN EXAMPLE

If you want to encourage deliberate decision making, you must model it by remaining calm, patient, and reasonable. If your child is upset, try to draw out his feelings. You can say, "Before we talk about what needs to happen, I would like to hear how you are feeling about it first." Parents who express empathy in response to intense feelings rather than engaging with their child on the same level of emotional intensity (which is like pouring gasoline on a fire) are effective at conflict resolution because the child appreciates that his feelings are their priority. A parent's concern and compassion for a child's feelings will encourage more constructive communication than will criticism of his conduct.

Impatient, critical, emotional, explosive, dictatorial parents are their own worst enemies in conflict with children, particularly during adolescence, when the teenager can start treating parents the same way they have been treating him.

In counseling, I have seen three types of parents who regularly model impulsive decision making in conflict with their children.

- Anger-prone parents have a very low tolerance for opposition because it defies their authority. They are highly controlling, highly judgmental, and take everything their child says or does as a personal affront. To reduce their vulnerability to impulsive decision making, they must learn to give up some control. *I don't have to have it all my way.* They must become less judgmental. *I don't have to always be right.* And they must take behavior they find offensive less personally. *Not everyone who offends me is out to get me.*
- Stress-prone parents have a very low tolerance for conflict because it requires too much energy. They are burdened by the constant pressure of overdemand, by waiting until the last minute to get things done, and by not investing in healthy self-care. They are usually worn down and wound up, with a negative attitude nourished by chronic fatigue and ongoing tension. To reduce their vulnerability to impulsive decision making, they have to set limits, accomplish tasks in a more timely way, and invest in more adequate self-maintenance, such as getting adequate sleep.
- Substance abuse–prone parents have a very low tolerance for opposition because it interferes with their chemically enhanced self-preoccupation. They regularly self-medicate to escape pain or seek pleasure, and everything else, including the children, takes second place. The parent who drinks too much, for example, is less governed by judgment, reason, and perspective and is often irritable, provocative, and argumentative. To reduce their vulnerability to impulsive decision making, these parents need to practice moderation or abstinence, joining a support group or getting professional help if they cannot do it on their own.

There is another kind of emotional arousal, in which people who hate arguing express the discomfort they feel by laughing or smiling nervously. Parents who grew up in households where conflict was discouraged often mask emotional arousal this way. Now the child feels that he is an object of amusement, just when he has gathered the courage to take on his parent. To have a powerful adult smile or laugh at you can feel humiliating and infuriating to a child, particularly an adolescent, who interprets it as disrespect. He feels put down for standing up for himself. This adds a new frustration, "I hate it when you laugh at me!" The lesson is simply this: *Do not laugh or smile when in conflict with your child, even if his challenge makes you feel anxious.* It signals to him that you do not take his concerns seriously.

ASSESS YOUR CHILD'S MOOD

Just as there are types of parents who are prone to impulsive decision making, certain physiological and psychological conditions can make children vulnerable to impulsiveness. It is worthwhile determining your child's mood before engaging in conflict with him. By ministering to his state of mind before conflict, you can reduce your child's emotional upset.

The model for this comes from Alcoholics Anonymous (AA), which encourages recovering alcoholics to maintain *emotional sobriety* so they don't put their substance sobriety at risk. I define emotional sobriety as a state in which feelings are honestly acknowledged and openly expressed but not allowed to do a person's thinking for them. It is critical for people in recovery to learn emotional sobriety because addictive behavior supports the habit of immediate gratification and impulsive decision making, of giving in to urgent wants and feelings no matter how self-destructive. In addition to supporting abstinence, the twelve-step program teaches people in recovery to resist the urgings of impulse and emotion, to delay action for thought, to consult better judgment before making decisions.

AA uses the acronym HALT: Never let yourself get Hungry, Angry, Lonely, or Tired. I have given this advice to parents of a sensitive or volatile child to help them reduce his emotional explosiveness. "Before you enter into disagreement with him about chores," I suggest, "check out his physical and psychological condition. Is he irritable from being hungry? If so, give him a snack before you set him to work. Is he aggrieved from already being angry? If so, listen to what recently happened at school that he still feels frustrated or resentful about. Is he feeling disconnected, anxious, and lonely? If so, take a few minutes to do something fun together. Is he cranky because he is tired? If so, let him rest." Conditions that commonly contribute to a child's lack of well-being, such as hunger, anger, loneliness, and being tired, can increase the likelihood of conflict. It behooves us as parents to heed that piece of folk wisdom "Don't pull the tail of the tiger." Parents must be mature and sensitive enough to know not to argue when either they or the child is upset and emotion rules the moment. *When we are upset, acting on what feels right can do a lot of wrong.* Sometimes judicious timing, waiting for feelings to settle down, finding out what those feelings are, can pay big dividends by encouraging the child's cooperation.

THE IMPORTANCE OF DELAY

There should be some rules that govern family conflicts. One is to have a *separation agreement* that everybody understands. A separation agreement is based on the principle of *delay*. What separates deliberate from impulsive decision making is the refusal to be ruled by the "tyranny of now." Creating a delay—call it "counting to ten" or "taking a timeout" or "creating an interrupt"—stops a torrent of emotionally driven words and actions and gives your child (and you) space to think. You might say, "I know what I *feel* like doing (or saying), I know what I *want* to do (or say), but I am going to take the time to consider what I really value, what I believe is appropriate, what I judge is wise." In the words of one psychologist: "Time-outs aren't just for kids! When parents are upset with their toddler and sense they are losing control, they should give themselves a timeout to settle down and rethink what is happening. Parents who are becoming upset because they can't control their toddler should give *themselves* a time-out to settle down and rethink what is happening."[9] This applies to older children, too. But don't forget the rule of separation. Establish a time to get back together and continue the discussion in more measured terms so no one feels that either the issue or relationship is being abandoned.

Parents can be caught off guard when an intense adolescent is pressing to resolve a disagreement so he can do something or go somewhere *right now.* But you are not locked in to that emotional moment. If your high school student tells you that she "has to have" permission and money to go to a concert this weekend, rather than fight it out now, you can break tension and slow decision making down. "Give me a separation for now and then we'll talk some more tonight, because this does sound like something important to discuss. I am not walking out on you; I just need time to think." Sometimes it's the teenager who exercises better judgment. At the point where her parents are getting angrier and she is also ready to explode, the daughter may choose to walk away to break the tension and calm down: "We need to talk about this later when we're not upset. I'm going to my room." Sometimes the parent refuses to give his daughter the timeout. "Where are you going? Don't you turn your back on me! Don't you dare walk away until I'm finished with you!" But she is already in her bedroom, with the door closed. Infuriated, the parent follows after and pushes open her door, yelling, "This argument will end when I am done talking and not before!" Now, denied the cooling off she was seeking, she screams at him. "You have no right to burst into my room like that. Get out! I hate you." Unhappily, in this situation, there is little chance for mending. They both say things they will later regret, may apologize for, but can never take back.

If this family had had a separation agreement, there might have been a better outcome. This agreement essentially says that when anyone starts feeling so upset as to be on the verge of doing or saying something he or she might regret, that person has the right to declare a timeout. A separation agreement includes the *two rules of delay.*

- When emotional intensity escalates to a potentially destructive point, either party has the right to deescalate the emotion by calling for a temporary interruption, a "ceasefire," which *the other party must respect.*

- At this point or later, when things are calmer, that party has a *responsibility* to arrange a mutually agreed upon time to resume the discussion of the disagreement.

Delay is only meant to defer the discussion of disagreement; it should never be used as a way to ignore or avoid it.

Without a separation agreement that both parent and child will honor, it is inevitable that they will end up popping off with ill-considered words or actions. When this happens, taking time to think after the fact must supplant thinking that did not occur before. Now reflection can beget correction. The offending party can ask himself: "If I were in this situation again, how could I avoid responding emotionally the way I did?" A lot of important learning in life comes after the fact for those people with the honesty and courage to look back and mine the good lessons that bad mistakes teach. At issue is not allowing impulsive decision making to emotionally dictate the conduct of the argument, particularly when a child uses tantrums or a parent uses yelling as a tactic to prevail.

A CHILD'S TANTRUMS AND A PARENT'S YELLING

Very young children throw temper tantrums for one or more of three reasons.

- The child needs *to release pent up emotion*—her frustration from feeling inadequately understood, stressed by family circumstances, or physically unwell. The main thing to remember about the tantrum is that the child is feeling genuinely upset. Provide an empathetic and calming response that allows the child to feel accepted and connected to you at a hard emotional time. The preverbal child can be held and cradled. The verbal child can be encouraged to use her "feeling words" ("hurt," "sad," "mad," "scared," "lonely," for example) to describe what is going on.
- The child wants *to command attention* from parents to divert it from the conflict. Clamor and drama can be used to redirect parents' attention

from the issue the child doesn't want to confront or be confronted with. Or they can help the child reclaim attention from whoever or whatever is currently occupying center stage in the family. The main thing to remember is that you may need to teach your child that you sometimes have to pay attention to other things, and it is okay. You will talk to him as soon as you are finished with what you are doing. Also explain how the child's loudness makes it harder for you to pay attention to him. "When you shout, I can't understand what you're saying for the noise you are making. If you want me to listen and understand, you must speak more quietly."

- The child wants *to force agreement* from parents by overwhelming them with an extreme expression of emotion. This behavior is usually calculated, not entirely impulsive. You may feel particularly self-conscious or embarrassed when a tantrum happens in public, and it can be tempting to give in just to quiet him down. The main thing to remember in this situation is the child isn't losing control of his emotions; he is using emotion to control you. You must therefore hold firm to whatever limit or rule you made. In actions or words, you must say and mean: "No matter how upset you act, it is not going to change my mind."

Parents must be prepared to make an empathetic response to any tantrum, to insist on quiet communication, and to refuse to change their position in the face of emotional upset. Since children most commonly throw tantrums in the early years of life, parents should teach the feeling words so that the child learns to describe her emotional states. Discussing feelings, parent to child and child to parent, allows your child to learn how to process emotional experience and to talk out difficult feelings instead of acting them out—by having a tantrum.

When a child yells and loses emotional control, we call it "throwing a tantrum." When parents yell at the child to get him to do what they want, I believe they are also throwing a tantrum. Both tantrums are a good example of what can happen in conflict when child or parent can no longer tolerate delay. They want to release emotion, get attention, or get a result *now*. As one parent in counseling described it, "When I get pushed too far I reach a breaking point. I just can't take what's going on anymore, and I lose it. I get loud so I can get the kids' attention. Now they know I'm serious, which I can tell because they're looking scared, like maybe I'm going to hit them. Of course I never would." But I disagree. "You have already 'hit' them. Threatening violence is a form of violence," I say. "Any time you are about to reach your breaking point, take a timeout. Set a time for further discussion, separate, cool down, and then start over to deal more calmly with whatever was going on."

Many tantrums, whether by parent or child, are similar to what one psychologist terms "emotional hijacking" or what one of his sources calls emotional "flooding," a state in which emotional intensity overrules rational thought and dictates impulsive action. "People who are flooded cannot hear without distortion or respond with clearheadedness; they find it hard to organize their thinking and fall back on *primitive reactions....* They just want things to stop, or want to run or, sometimes, to strike back.... At this point—full hijacking—a person's emotions are so intense, their perspective is so narrow, and their thinking so confused that there is no hope of taking the other's viewpoint or settling things in a reasonable way."[10] Now only yelling will do, yet parental yelling is counterproductive; it does more harm than good. Yelling is not talking out what is wanted; it is acting out to get one's way. Consider just a few of the unproductive outcomes.

- A loud, angry voice is threatening, a possible precursor to verbal or physical violence.
- The child who is yelled at can feel angry, hurt, or frightened and unsafe.
- What parents model is what they teach: yelling teaches yelling.
- When parents lose emotional control to get control, the child ends up in control, able to provoke parents to an extreme response.
- Constant parental yelling sets up *yelling cycles*: now the child waits to be yelled at before complying, while parents yell when they grow impatient with delay.
- The message parents want to send is obscured by the intensity and volume of emotion they express.

- Parental yelling undercuts respect for parental authority. Resorting to yelling only bankrupts a parent's more rational powers of persuasion.
- Parents who say, "You make me so angry, that's why I yell!" have just handed over the keys to their emotional control to the child.

If a child gives in to parental yelling, he is at risk of developing self-contempt for not speaking up for himself and demanding to be respectfully treated. Thus parental mistreatment can lead to a child who is driven by fear and unable to assert himself. This pattern may carry through to his adult relationships later on.

How to recover from a pattern of yelling? In an earlier book, I suggested that parents calmly and insistently pursue what they want instead. I encourage them to recover from yelling by going to the other extreme. Talking more softly can be very effective because the child does not expect this response. In addition, he must now listen carefully to what you are saying. This creates a new cue for seriousness. Now he knows the parent means business because she has lowered her voice.[11]

But what about raised voices in those unpredictable emotional outbursts that can occur over seemingly insignificant events, overreactions that blow in like a storm out of nowhere that catch everyone, including the exploder, unprepared?

OVERREACTIONS

Sudden emotional outbursts often seem inexplicable and unjustified because they seem far out of proportion to the event that triggered them. The target of the overreaction objects: "All I said was..." "All I did was..." "All that happened was...and you just lost it! What's the matter with you?" Now the target feels as hurt and angry as the exploder may feel foolish and regretful.

A common response to an overreaction is for the parties involved, the person exploding and the bystander or person exploded at, to put the unpleasant episode behind them and decide not to talk about it. This is a mistake: The seemingly minor issues that set off such intense emotional reactions are actually major issues in disguise. Disproportionate emotional responses are always worth trying to understand. Usually, one of four kinds of overreactions has been at play. There are overreactions that occur as a function of suppression, similarity, symbolism, and surprise.

Overreactions based on suppression occur when an incident feels like the last straw. After a series of frustrations, irritations, or hurts, the person feels like she can't take any more, and then some additional upset comes her way. At this point, the overreaction ventilates built-up emotion that may not have been adequately identified or openly discussed in previous offenses. The explosion essentially says, "This is just too much!" To begin to understand this kind of overreaction, the person needs to identify what other hardships have been going on.

Overreactions based on similarity occur when an incident is a painful reminder of something that has happened before. At this point, the overreaction protests the repetition of what the person dearly wished would never recur. The explosion essentially says, "This is just like before!" To begin to understand this kind of overreaction, the person needs to identify how past pain has been revived by what feels like a replay of an old event.

Overreactions based on symbolism occur when an incident represents a theme in the person's life, signifying some abiding issue that continues to cause them pain. The explosion essentially says, "This just goes to show that nothing's changed!" To begin to understand this kind of overreaction, the person needs to identify this theme and explore the feelings that the offending episode represented.

Overreactions based on surprise occur when an incident was not only unwanted, but, more important, was unexpected. The explosion essentially says, "I didn't think this was going to happen!" To begin to understand this kind of overreaction, the person needs to examine what he was anticipating and how it felt to be caught unprepared.

Because overreactions can be so emotionally costly, they are worth the effort and expense it takes to understand why they occurred. This learning can decrease the likelihood of that kind of outburst happening again.[12]

The rule is: Don't let overreactions pass without taking time afterwards to profit from the education they offer. In conflict, it is as good to be self-aware as it is to be sensitive to the emotions of others. However, it is *not* good to use strong emotion to manipulate the other party—as a ploy to get what you want.

EMOTIONAL EXTORTION

The language of emotion is often expressed nonverbally, especially in conflict. As one psychologist writes, "Nonverbal communication behaviors reveal much about people's affective responses to conflict, perhaps more than verbal communication."[13] Starting when their children are as young as four of five years old and through adolescence, parents can find themselves under powerful emotional onslaught when the boy or girl finds that being reasonable will not prevail.

There are a number of common *emotional tactics* that a young person may put into play when explanation or argument is causing conflict to go the parent's way. Sometimes the son or daughter will act so *loving* that a parent cannot resist pleasure from this show of consideration and approval, and relents on that account. Sometimes the young person will act so *angry*, loudly or silently, that the parent will give in to relieve painful feelings of rejection. Sometimes *criticism* from a son or daughter will sway a parent who cannot bear appearing incompetent or inadequate in the young person's eyes. Sometimes a young person's display of *suffering* (sadness or tears) will be more than a guilty parent can withstand. Sometimes seeing a son or daughter act like a *helpless* victim of the adult's decision can cause a parent to take pity on the young person and relax a rule they were contesting. Sometimes having a son or daughter express *apathy* can influence an insecure parent who fears abandonment of caring in their relationship. And sometimes a young person's *explosiveness* can create a sense of physical threat that intimidates the parent into giving in.

What psychologist John Narciso calls "get-my-way behavior,"[14] I call "emotional extortion,"[15] and therapist Susan Forward calls "emotional blackmail." She defines it as "a powerful form of manipulation in which people close to us threaten, either directly or indirectly, to punish us if we don't do what they want. At the heart of any kind of blackmail is a threat, which can be expressed in many different ways: *If you don't behave the way I want you to, you will suffer....* Emotional blackmailers know how much we value our relationship with them. They know our vulnerabilities.... When they fear they won't get their way, they use this intimate knowledge to shape the threats that give them the payoff they want: our compliance."[16] You need to know what your emotional vulnerabilities are, because your child knows them well. She knows just which emotional strings to pull to get her way. To forestall the success of these tactics, rank the following emotional manipulations from those you find most to those you find least hard to resist:

- when my child acts loving,
- when my child is angry with me,
- when my child criticizes me,
- when my child suffers,
- when my child acts helpless,
- when my child shows apathy, and
- when my child's behavior is explosive.

By being clear about your particular emotional vulnerabilities, you can prepare and protect yourself the next time emotional extortion comes your way. You can respond like the parent who refuses to be bullied by her loud, angry teenage son: "When you are through acting angry, I am willing to discuss with you, calmly and reasonably, what you want. Not before." *Always turn emotional extortion into rational discussion.* And of course, parents must resist using emotional extortion themselves.

There can be gender role differences. Men may use anger to elicit fear, while women may suffer to elicit guilt. The man's manipulative expression of anger implies a threat: "If you don't let me have my way, there is no telling what I will do!" The woman's manipulative expression of suffering is an attempt to evoke compassion or guilt: "You are hurting my feelings. I feel sad, and it's your fault. You owe it to me to give me my way!" But not succumbing to emotional extortion does not mean that you should ignore feelings in conflict. On the contrary, feelings should be *declared* in order to communicate about your emotional state, but they should never be used for manipulative gain.

How can you tell whether the child's expression of strong emotion in conflict is a true expression of feelings and not a manipulative ploy? If the child's emotion subsides in response to your empathetic listening, his feelings were probably honestly meant. One danger of emotional manipulation is that it can corrupt the true meaning of honest feeling by creating distrust. So a parent to whom a child repeatedly says "I love you" to motivate parental permission can come to distrust the child's expression of love when it is truly meant. Tired of being softened up this way, the parent asks, "What do you want this time?" Or the parent who continually expresses suffering to manipulate his child with guilt can generate similar distrust when honest suffering is expressed and only empathy is wanted. Now it's the child's turn to ask, "What do you want this time?" The more an emotion is used to manipulate, the less authentic value others place on the expression of that emotion.

And beware the strong-willed child or prickly mid-adolescent who uses emotional bluster to get parents who are bringing up an issue the child doesn't want to deal with to back off. The *protective belligerence* conveyed by irritability or a dramatically displayed bad mood should not deter parents from discussions and encounters that need to occur.

ANGER

Anger is probably the most important emotion to monitor in conflict because of the potential for aggression. Parents must be able to constructively manage their own anger so they can teach a child to do the same. Anger can be particularly threatening to a very young child because it interrupts the expression of loving feelings—parent to child and child to parent. It can feel alienating, lonely, and frightening. The child must learn that anger is only temporary. It takes experiencing some normal anger to and from the parent in conflict before the child comes to understand that this is a passing emotional discomfort, not any permanent loss of love. Parents can assure both the strong-willed child and the adolescent: "No matter how angry we may get at each other, our love will be there when the anger has gone away."

And when correcting a child, never do it in anger, for two reasons. First, the consequence you impose is likely to be so extreme you will have to retract or at least modify it later, showing your child that you don't mean what you say. "You're grounded for the next year!" explodes the father whose teenage son has taken out the family car without permission, only to reduce the sentence to a week after he has calmed down. Second, anger can obscure the problem being corrected because the parents' intense emotion becomes the most salient message the child receives. If you ask her why she was punished, she will say, "Because my parents were angry at me." Ask her, "What for?" and she will answer, "I don't know. They were just yelling at me like they always do!" So the child misses the point about not leaving the back door open and allowing the dog to escape again. *In conflict, the issues are often too important to get extremely angry about.*

Parents can help their child put anger in emotional context by explaining how the basic functions of all emotions are the same: registering the felt awareness of an event (sadness over a loss, for example) and motivating a response (grief, for example) to that event. Each emotion commonly arises in response to a different kind of experience. For example, frustration is a typical response to the thwarting of desires or needs, fear is a typical response to danger, and surprise is a typical response to the unexpected.

The function of anger is to identify violations. Anger is evaluative; it comes into play when we judge that we have been *wronged*. It then motivates us to make some expressive, protective, or corrective response, sometimes precipitating conflict that is fought to set things right.

Consider the mother who feels very angry that her teenage daughter wore her watch, a prized anniversary gift from her husband, without asking, and then returned it damaged. How will she manage her sense of violation? Already on the defensive, the teenager awaits the expected attack, ready to justify her actions, "I was only *borrowing* it. How was I supposed to know you'd mind?" and to protest: "I didn't break it, someone else did!"

But this mother doesn't fall into the attack-and-defend trap because she knows two important anger management rules. First, she knows that people only get angry about what matters to them, so *anger is always about caring*. Second, she knows that by translating her anger into *a statement of caring*, she is more likely to encourage a discussion about what happened and to reach an acceptable resolution.

So she says something like: "Of course I feel angry about what happened to my watch, but that is not what I want to talk with you about. What I care about is how you treat me and my belongings. In the future, please ask first when you want something of mine, and take good care of what I let you use. As for what happened this time, we need to figure out how you can pay me back for the cost of repair." *If you can practice turning feelings of anger against someone into statements about what, in the situation, really matters to you, you can sensibly resolve a lot of conflicts.* You can also use anger as a cue to examine more sensitive feelings that the anger may be concealing. Do this by asking yourself: "What am I feeling besides anger?" Anger is frequently used as armor; it is a protective "cover emotion" (particularly for men) that conceals more vulnerable feelings that we may want to hide from ourselves or keep hidden from others. In counseling, when tempers escalate between one father and his teenage daughter, I put this question to him: "What else are you feeling besides anger?" My inquiry apparently catches him off guard. He bursts into tears, revealing his sadness over the hostility that has grown between them. But if he is surprised by his display of emotion, his daughter is shocked, exclaiming, "Dad, are you okay? I've never seen you cry before!" And the emotional tone of the entire interaction changes. The father's grief over his loss is revealed, and his daughter, who until now didn't know how much he cared, feels gratitude.

Try asking yourself the same question when you feel angry. If the answer is, "I am also feeling sad," or, "I'm also feeling anxious," for example, then take the time to reflect on those emotions or talk about what that sadness or anxiety is. The benefit of this exercise is to clarify and amplify what is emotionally going on for yourself and for others. If parent or child thinks that all the other ever gets in conflict is angry, then valuable emotional information will never be revealed or discussed. Conflict creates an opportunity for more communication if parent and child allow themselves to disclose more, which includes allowing themselves to be more emotionally known.

People who feel *obliged to please others* or *entitled to get their way* can become angry in conflict for the same reason: their wants are denied. They may become angry when they fail to please, as being in disagreement with the other person implies. And they can become angry when disagreement opposes their desire to prevail. In both cases, their "sense of should" has been violated. "I 'should' have pleased the other person," says the pleaser. "I 'should' have gotten what I wanted," thinks the entitled person. The only solution to people of either predisposition is to learn to substitute the word "want" for "should," gradually coming to accept that getting their wants satisfied just some of the time is good enough: "I want to please you all the time, but I know no matter how hard I try, I really can't."

If you come under angry attack from your child and are on the receiving end of deliberately hurtful words, it is generally better not to respond in kind because that will just build more anger between you. Instead, pause, create a quiet space in the communication, then make an empathetic response. Beneath violent language there are often vulnerable feelings, so see whether you can shift your focus of concern to those: "I know you wouldn't say that unless you were feeling really upset with me, can you tell me what those feelings are?" If you can get the child to share his feelings instead of hurling insults at you, you change his view of you from enemy to concerned, compassionate friend. Then it is your turn to express your feelings, declaring that you need for him not to attack you verbally again. Now you can get back to the original issue and try to resolve it in a calmer way.

I am not proposing that emotions should be either ignored or suppressed, including the unhappy emotions that are aroused in the normal course of family conflict. Because they yield significant information about one's psychological state in conflict, I believe they should be attended to. They should be safely expressed so they can be acknowledged. They should be talked about so they are not acted out.

They should be personally owned, not blamed on others. In addition, feelings should be enlisted as agents of sensitivity, enabling both parties to empathetically connect with each other. The power of the empathetic response is to interrupt tension from argument by shifting focus to the other person's well-being in the emotional moment. Instead of debating why the other person is wrong, you express concern for how the other person is feeling. So when your upset five-year-old objects to your decision that he can't play with friends until he picks up his room, rather than defend your choice in an argument, you make a request. "Before we talk about this any further, please tell me how you are feeling." In many cases, expressing concern for the child not only defuses conflict, but ends up eliciting cooperation because the child knows you care.

The role of emotion in conflict is to create awareness and to express sensitivity; it should not be given the "authority." Feelings are very good informants but very bad advisors. To borrow advice from Alcoholics Anonymous, when in conflict maintain emotional sobriety and deliberate decision making by committing to the following aphorism: "THINK... THINK... THINK."

THREE IDEAS ABOUT *EMOTION AND CONFLICT* TO CARRY FORWARD

- Because opposition can generate intense feelings, the first priority in any family conflict is the safe management of emotional arousal so no one says or does anything they will have cause to regret later.
- Because the future welfare of family relationships is at stake, the way conflict is conducted (the communication and tactics used) must always be more important than the outcome (the resolution reached).
- Because of the intensity of the emotions that are aroused in conflict, empathetic response to each other's feelings is the best way to keep unhappy emotion from dictating harsh words and hurtful actions.

3

COMMUNICATION AND CONFLICT

Because what family members know about each other's life experience depends mostly on what they tell each other, communication is what it takes to keep everyone adequately informed. Insufficient sharing of information, using spoken language to careless or deceitful effect, "misreading" the other person's mind, can cause misunderstanding and estrangement in families. Thus every conflict provides an opportunity for needed communication to occur. Think of it this way.

CONFLICT AS A CHANCE TO COMMUNICATE

When family members are in conflict, it means that something within them or between them is worth talking about. Not talking about things that bother them creates tension in the form of silent discomfort between parent and child. The relationship becomes strained or abrasive until what is being withheld is finally declared and discussed. The ten-year-old admits that the reason he has been hard to talk to is that he has been lying about keeping up with his homework. He feels fearful of being found out. Or the parent admits, "The reason I've been fussing at you about not wasting food and money is that there have been changes at work and I'm worried about losing my job." Conflict can be informative.

Disagreement offers two opposing ways of considering the same issue. Clothes that a teenager thinks look "cool" can seem scandalous to her parents. Exchanging opinions allows each party to see the other person's point of view and be informed by that perspective. Conflict has an upside if the participants are willing to learn from each other, and if they can put aside power struggles and instead address the questions that conflicts are always really about.

- What really occurred? (Past issues)
- What is happening? (The current disagreement)
- What will happen? (The desired outcome)

Each party agrees to disagree over the answers to these questions. The outcome of any conflict is uncertain at the outset. Parent and child begin with conflicting points of view and end with a mutual understanding that provides a resolution both parties are willing to accept. Here are a few *conflict questions* that people frequently fight about:

- Who is responsible?
- Who goes first?
- Who gets what?
- Who gets most?
- Who did what?
- Who does most?
- What's appropriate?
- When must it be done?
- How should it be done?
- Who started it?
- How can we agree?
- What is best?
- Which way is right?
- What is fair?
- What really happened?
- Why did it happen?

In counseling, I have found it useful to help family members reframe conflicts from *power struggles* to be won to *questions* to be answered. This helps to replace attacking and defending with discussing and understanding. I tell them, "See if you can restate your conflict in terms of a question or questions and then try to come up with answers. If you can find mutually acceptable answers in your discussion, you will have settled your disagreement. This is what I will try to help you do." By reframing a disagreement as a question, people can discuss it more dispassionately.

Parents are often in conflict over who has to play the bad cop in getting children to do their chores. "You nag them too much!" accuses one parent. "I have to do *all* the supervision!" accuses the other. They throw charges at each other and resentment builds. Then I interrupt and suggest they try using questions instead of accusations. What are the major questions at issue? We can usually come up with four. First, do they want children to do chores? Yes. Second, what are the most important chores for children to do? They can usually agree on several. Third, if the children resist, what strategies can they use to encourage them? Some supervision in the form of reminding, but also making use of the television, the computer, video games, or other household entertainment conditional upon completion of chores. Fourth, who will enforce the rule? Each parent will usually commit to keeping after a particular child to accomplish specific chores. With these answers, they have created some certainty they did not have before, and settled this particular conflict, at least for the present.

Ongoing uncertainty about what is going on within each other and in each other's lives is what keeps us gathering information. Questions are a primary communication tool to satisfy our abiding curiosity. Ignorance about each other cannot be avoided, but we can only tolerate so much. When that curiosity cannot be satisfied and uncertainty about what the other person is thinking or feeling rules, a serious exposure to conflict is created.

IGNORANCE AND UNCERTAINTY

Family members know each other intimately, but there will always be a part of each person that is secret. Family members are also strangers in the sense that what other family members are feeling and thinking at any moment in time is invisible. We cannot read each other's minds. To complicate matters further, how honestly we share information with others depends on how honest we are with ourselves (we could be out of touch or in denial), and how open we want to be (we might lie to mislead, to protect privacy, or to preserve secrecy.)

Inadequate communication between family members creates a variety of problems: misunderstanding, estrangement, distrust, suspicion, and insecurity, among others. I see it often in family counseling: More conflict results from what people do not communicate than from what they do, from "shutting up" instead of "speaking up." Open discussion has a chance of creating understanding, but ignorance allows a host of false assumptions to grow.

A major function of verbal communication for family members is to reduce the abiding ignorance between them. Exchanging honest information about our feelings and thoughts and behaviors, family members stay connected. Parent and child need to

- send data (talk about themselves),
- receive data (listen to the other person),
- request data (ask questions to get information), and
- respond to requests for data (answer questions about themselves).

You need to model all four functions to encourage the child to learn to do the same. When someone is not an adequate talker, listener, asker, or responder, communication breaks down. Four classic communication problems follow. "You won't talk to me!" "You aren't listening to me!" "You didn't ask me!" and "You don't answer me!" When you hear yourself or your child uttering any of these complaints, you know there is a communication gap between you.

In families, ignorance about each other is the continuing problem that communication is meant to overcome. This problem is ongoing because no matter how much you and your children know about each other today, tomorrow brings new experiences and perspectives. It takes an enormous investment in communication to keep a family functioning together as a unit, to keep everyone "on the same page" and "in the know." Of course, this knowledge is only as good as it is true, which is why so many family conflicts are about determining what the truth really is.

THE PROBLEM WITH TRUTH

When parent and child communicate, they want to trust that they are being told the truth. But truth in this world is very hard to come by. For example, when parents confront a miscreant child, they often want answers to three basic questions:

- What happened? (They want a *description* of what occurred.)
- How did it happen? (They want to know the sequence of events that the child can *recall*.)
- Why did it happen? (They want an explanation of *cause*.)

The problem is that description depends upon perception, which is highly individual; recall depends on memory, which is selective; and fixing causation is always complex. Just ask two siblings to describe their most recent fight, charging them to come up with a single answer to the following question upon which both agree: "Who started it?" Asking this question usually reinvigorates the conflict because neither child describes what happened the same way, remembers the same sequence of events, attributes the conflict to the same cause, or assigns the same instigator responsibility. They can't even agree on exactly when and why it began. So don't ask your children, "Who started it?" unless you want to start another argument between them.

Establishing truth in communication is not some abstract philosophical problem; it is a pressing psychological need that is always frustrated by ignorance. Parents learn the hard way to make decisions based on less truth than they would ideally like. What started the fight this time? Was it an ugly word spoken today, some lingering grievance left over from a past quarrel, or a current expression of the historical rivalry that began the day the second child was born? All we know for sure is that we are tired of their bickering, so we send them to their rooms to play alone. Compounding this challenge is an additional constraint—in the family, a variety of communication needs must be managed simultaneously.

INFORMATION NEEDS IN COMMUNICATION

This motivation for communication is based on satisfying at least four different information needs.

- The need to know, to be informed. "Talk to me. Tell me what's going on."
- The need not to know, to be unaware. "Please don't talk about that. I don't want to know."
- The need to be known, to be understood. "Hear me out. Listen to what I have to say."
- The need not to be known, to be private. "Don't ask me. It's personal."

Consider what happens when you frustrate these needs.

- Deny the controlling parent or the anxious child his urgent need to know, and each may fight for information: "Tell me and tell me now!"
- Deny the busy parent who doesn't want to be bothered or the errant child who doesn't want to be confronted her need not to know, and each may fight for ignorance. "Not now, let me alone!"
- Deny the long-suffering parent who loves to complain or the self-centered child who loves to show off her need to be known, and each may fight for an audience. "I'm not through with what I have to say!"
- Deny the parent who is hiding an addiction or the self-conscious early teen who is entering puberty his need not to be known, and each may fight for secrecy: "That's none of your business!"

Or consider how one person's need for information can conflict with another's.

- The need to be informed can conflict with the need for privacy. A single parent wants to keep dating information to himself, while his child wonders how serious this new relationship is becoming.
- One parent's need to be informed can conflict with the other's need to be unaware. A highly involved mother may want a lot of detail about what's going on in her children's lives, while her uninvolved husband may prefer to let them be.

The best resolution of such conflicts is compromise, with each party agreeing to settle for "enough" information. This might be more than one party wants to share, but less than the other would ideally want to know. Such a working compromise is commonly made between parents and their teenager. They accept being less informed than they like and he submits to being better known than he wants to be.

You need to be particularly sensitive to the way information needs change during the mercurial adolescent years. If you find yourself often wondering why communication with your thirteen-year-old has become so difficult, take it as an opportunity to assess how you are responding to her communication needs.

- Does she need more information from you, for example, about what are normal physical and emotional changes that come with puberty?
- Does she need less information from you about rising tensions between you and your spouse or between you and your ex-husband?
- Does her emotional turmoil from being in love for the first time need to be better understood?
- Does she need to be more private, for the sake of her newfound independence, about all the wilder things her friends at middle school are now talking about?

As our children grow, we have to keep talking, openly communicating so we can sensitively manage our children's multiple, ever-changing information needs. It always helps to say something like this: "Whenever you need more information from me, whenever you feel I am telling you too much, whenever you need me to understand you better, or whenever you want me to give you more privacy, please say so, and we can talk." Talking is the all-purpose communication tool.

WHY COMMUNICATE?

Verbal communication does come down to being willing to talk, to speak up, and knowing that it is possible to feel emotionally safe, as described in Chapter Two. In counseling, however, a teenager—even though she lives in a loving family—will sometimes elect not to communicate with her parents because, in her view, there is no point. "They can't understand me..." or "They don't agree with me..." or "They won't do what I want...so I don't say anything." I try to explain that none of these three frustrations has anything to do with the primary purpose of communication, which is *to honor her right of and responsibility for self-expression.* She needs to go on record, to make herself known. Parental understanding, agreement, and consent are secondary gains. She may need to engage in an argument with them to try to influence their thinking. She cannot expect her parents to be sensitive to her opinions, needs, and wants if she refuses to speak up. And parents are not immune to similar misunderstanding. They don't always know what constitutes listening, either. So when their child doesn't do as directed, they may angrily accuse him of not listening to them, to which he may honestly—and accurately—reply: "I did too listen to what you said; I just didn't do what you wanted!"

One rule that encourages speaking up is that all parties must listen without interrupting, correcting, criticizing, or otherwise discouraging communication and allow each family member the *right to have a full say.* It takes patient listening to invite full participation in conflict. In my practice I often see young children stop talking because impatient parents cut them off and shut them down.

The worst is the parent who seems to suffer from a *listening disability.* This doesn't mean being unable to hear; it means being unwilling to listen. She is often so focused on talking about herself that she can't see beyond her own self-interest; she is "deaf" to any voice but her own. The most attention she can give to others is to complain, criticize, correct, or direct. In counseling, her daughter complains, "There's no way to talk to my mom because she does all the talking. She's not interested in what I have to say. The only person she listens to is herself." This is a parent with a high need to be known by others, but a low need to know much about them. The lesson is pretty simple. *If you want your child to talk and listen to you, particularly in conflict, then listen to your child.* Listening shows your child that you respect what he has to say.

Sometimes, however, a teenager will deliberately go on strike, refusing to communicate in order to keep parents in the dark about her life. This sets up a conflict between their need to know and her need to be unknown, between their request for conversation and her refusal to talk. So what can parents do to bring her to the discussion table? Do not fight with her to get her to talk, but do hold her responsible for the consequences of not talking. The parent can say, "Whether or not to talk to me about your life is up to you. However, I do need to say that not talking to me may not work well for you because it doesn't work for me. This is what goes through my mind. First I feel ignorant and wonder what is going on. Then I begin to worry about you. That's when I start asking myself: What if something's seriously wrong? Then I answer my question by imagining the worst: You are in some kind of danger or trouble that you are trying to hide. Wanting to protect you from this unknown harm, I decide to restrict your freedom. I don't let you go anywhere and I don't give you any money. You may get angry at me for setting limits based on unfounded ideas. You tell me that my thinking is completely off base. But how do I know? You wouldn't communicate, and I was just doing my best by you based on all the information I wasn't given. That's what can happen when you decide not to talk to me. My ignorance does you no favors. Of course, none of this would have to happen if you had kept me adequately informed. But, as I said, that is always up to you."[1]

Another way to open up a dialogue is to forsake spoken communication for the written kind. Leave a private note expressing your caring and concern in an envelope on your daughter's bed. Encourage her to write back if it suits her. By separating the message from the messenger and giving her time to read and think about what you've written, you signify your willingness to listen when she is ready.

Today, the number of ways we can communicate with our children has increased dramatically, thanks to the information technology we have at our command. After all, now we can trace where in the virtual world of the Internet our children go. We can have cell phone contact with them any time and check the phone memory and/or bill to see who is being called. We can even use a global positioning system to track where in the world our teenager drives. "What about my right to privacy?" an older child will object. To which the parent must be ready to explain that a child's privacy from parental intrusion is a privilege, not a right. "So long as you are behaving responsibly and keeping me adequately informed and remain open to discussion, privacy is yours.

However, if your behavior puts you at risk of harm and you will not talk to me about what's going on, then I will 'snoop and spy' as you call it, and invade your privacy to try to find out myself. I will do this for your safety's sake."

At first, many parents thought that these new communication devices would make it easier to keep up with their children's lives, with their teenagers in particular, who like to revive the old childhood game of hide and seek, "Find me if you can."

Actually, all this technology has provided little relief from parental ignorance, since the more we know, the more we want to know, and the more anxious we become when we realize how much we don't know. Now the conflict question that increasingly perplexes parents is, "Do we know enough?" One parent thought so. "Call me when you get back to your friend's house tonight," she tells her teenage daughter, who readily agrees and calls as promised. The problem, as trouble later revealed, was that she had been calling from her cell phone and was not where she said she was. Her parents then insisted that she call from friends' houses on a land line, so they could verify where the call was made from. Parents usually give a child a cell phone so they can reach him anytime. But sometimes he doesn't want to be reached, so he doesn't pick up. By now, most parents have avoided this conflict by simply setting a condition of use: If he wants a cell phone he will have to answers their calls. For every system of regulation and surveillance that parents impose, adolescents will try to find a way to circumvent it, perpetuating the ongoing conflict between *parent as rule maker* and *teenager as rule breaker.*

Parents need to encourage communication as best they can and hold their children accountable for not talking. At the same time, they must hold themselves accountable for *how* they talk, particularly during conflict, when impatience and emotion can cause them to change their manner of speech.

CONFLICT CAN ALTER SPOKEN LANGUAGE

In the heat of conflict, frustration and irritation can cause both parent and child to resort to *blaming* ("It's all your fault!" or the more extreme "You always…" or "You never…"). What happens is this: The disputants choose words that become more extreme, abstract, and evaluative. In counseling, I encourage parent and child to take joint responsibility for the disagreement, and I advise the accusing party to describe the other person's objectionable behavior as a "sometimes" thing. Blame and exaggeration are not only inaccurate; they are inflammatory. Statements of objectivity and moderation tend to cool things down.

For example, parents, frustrated with their nine-year-old's increasingly recalcitrant, pre-adolescent defiance, sit the young man down to tell him how they want him to behave around the house. "We just want you to be trustworthy, respectful, cooperative, helpful, and courteous, the way you used to be. We just want you to start being yourself and acting more grown-up. Is that clear?" To which the boy can honestly respond, "No, because you haven't told me what to do."

One of the most useful pieces of advice on this problem comes from psychologist John Narciso. He recommends that people forsake the use of general, judgmental labels and instead use specific words and phrases to describe what they want. He calls this using operational language. "An operational definition describes an event or happening."[2] For example, parents might say to the child, "Respect your elders," leaving the child to figure out what "respect" means. Using operational language, however, parents might say, "It is respectful to look at the person until they are done talking before you look away." They operationally define what they mean in terms of specific behaviors that are easy for a child to understand. Narciso writes, "When I communicate operationally, what I want to happen is clearer to all those involved."[3] Resist the temptation to make general, meaningless requests, such as:

- Behave yourself!
- Act your age!
- Stop being so messy!
- Be responsible!
- Talk nicely!

At most, such abstractions convey disapproval, which leaves a child feeling criticized without knowing exactly for what. This only increases her frustration: "I don't know what you mean and I don't know what you want!" We all have our own subjective definitions for "nicely," "messy," and "responsible." To a child, "Keep your room neat" may mean "Keep the mess out of sight." So he shoves it under the bed, under the sheets, or in the closet.

To the parent, "Keep your room neat" may mean "Keep everything picked up off the floor and in its place in a drawer, on the shelf, or hung on a hanger where it belongs." This confusion over meaning is how so many conflicts over room cleanup begin. "It *is* clean!" protests the child, having successfully hidden the mess. "It is *not* clean!" counters the parent, opening the closet door, exposing the hidden stash of jumbled belongings. Unless you define what you want operationally, the use of abstractions in conflict will only add to the confusion.

To make matters worse, the abstractions parents use are sometimes judgmental. "You are so irresponsible with your toys!" they say, by which they mean the child left one toy outside overnight to get rained on. "I am *not* irresponsible!" protests the child, by which he means he usually does remember to bring his playthings back inside at the end of the day. *The more abstractions are used to confront problems, the more conflicts of meaning are likely to be created.*

Evaluative abstractions that don't just categorize actions but also criticize the actor just add insult to injury. Not only is the child failing to understand what his parents mean; he is also failing to live up to some measure of character they value. "Irresponsible" is not an objective description or a term of endearment; it is name-calling, an insult. It is also counterproductive: Hurt another person's feelings, particularly a child's, and that person will likely want to hurt you back.

The lesson is simply this. When you feel tempted to use an abstract or evaluative label with your child, take the time to define what you want operationally instead. Do you feel inclined to accuse the child of not being cooperative? If so, specify the behavior you would consider cooperative. "We would like you to put the trash can out front every Thursday night before we have supper, without our having to remind you to do it." Do you feel like calling your teenager rude when she disagrees with you? If so, specify her rude behavior and operationally define the courteous behavior you would like to see. "Please don't interrupt or walk away when I am talking to you; I don't do that when you are talking to me." Do you repeatedly warn your six-year-old, "Behave yourself" when entering a supermarket? If so, operationally translate that instruction into specific conduct that you want. "Please talk quietly, leave items on the shelves, and walk beside me, don't run ahead of me, when we go down the aisles." Concrete communication is particularly important with young children. Providing clarity can prevent a lot of misunderstanding. Don't argue with a four-year-old about such abstract concepts as responsibility, courtesy, or honesty. Instead, talk about drying off a toy when it gets wet, thanking Aunt Ellen for the gift, or telling your teacher the truth about what happened.

The most destructive form of judgmental labeling is *name-calling*. Not only does it hurt the person being named, but the name-caller often feels justified in treating the other person accordingly. Your nine-year-old calls his younger brother an *idiot* and then proceeds to treat him like one. He makes fun of everything the younger boy says. Or the frustrated dad says to his academically unmotivated teenage daughter, "I give up on you! You'll never succeed in anything because you're just like all your *loser* friends!" And the man abandons this daughter and shifts more attention to her high-achieving younger sister. The no name-calling rule also applies to parents of younger children. The parent who can't stand it when his six-year-old cries over a lost toy should *not* say: "If you're going to act like a *cry baby*, then I'll really give you something to cry about!" Child abuse, cruel playground teasing, and the commission of most hate crimes depend on name-calling to pave the way to violence. Calling someone a hateful name can often motivate hateful treatment that follows. *This is how we treat trash like you!*

Name-calling can start very young. For example, the frustrated four-year-old yells at his mother, "You're a stupid-head!" and then slaps her in the face. In the angry moment, the child may believe that it is okay to hit a parent who is acting like a stupid-head. Now is a good time for a serious discussion about the power of name-calling, the harmful permission it can give, and acceptable alternatives for expressing anger. "When you are angry, tell me that you are and we can talk about it. But, please, no name-calling. It hurts my feelings, and it encouraged you to treat me in ways that we don't allow in this family. In this family, no one is allowed to hit anyone!"

It's worth keeping this riddle in mind: When they fight, what do humans and other animals have in common? Answer? They all fight with their mouths. But animals use sharp teeth; for people sharp words are the weapon of choice. We are all misled when we are young by the old adage that is still in play: "Sticks and stones can break my bones, but words can never hurt me." This is not true. In human conflict, words do most of the damage, and name-calling does the most damage of all.

In addition to forsaking the use of abstractions, labels, and judgments in conflict, parents may also want to limit the use of negative commands.

NEGATIVE COMMANDS

Stop that! Quit doing that! Don't do that again! Frustrated parents issue negative commands, and their child often responds by continuing the very action the parents want to discourage. Having been repeatedly warned before sitting down for supper not to spill his glass of milk, the four-year-old spills it anyway. "How often do I have to tell you *not* to spill?" screams the parent. "I hate supper time! You always yell at me!" cries the child, bursting into tears. Once again, dinnertime, which should be pleasant family time, is ruined for everyone.

There are four problems with negative commands. First, they set up negative expectations in the child's mind: *My parent thinks I'm going to spill again, so maybe I will.* Second, the action part of the command often carries more weight than the negative part, so the child discounts the "don't" and focuses on the "spill," obediently doing what the verb decrees. Third, with an oppositional or willful child, a negative command invites defiance. *By refusing to do what I'm told, I get to show I am in charge.* Fourth, the negative command at best interrupts and warns; it has little educational value since it doesn't present the child with a positive alternative.

This last point is extremely important to remember. Negative commands have no instructional power unless you also take the time to prescribe a more effective behavior instead. The parents of the child who spilled milk might say, "I'd like you to pick up your glass of milk with both hands because that way it will be more secure."

Worst are parents who routinely give negative commands when their child is about to embark on what should be a positive experience for her.

- Don't forget to call when you get there.
- Don't spend all your money.
- Don't go off with strangers.
- Don't be late getting home.

The child hears everything but "don't." The parent would have been better served by giving positive directions.

- Call me when you get there.
- Save ten dollars for emergencies.
- Stick with your friends.
- Get home by the time we agreed.

Or consider that classic parental complaint: "Stop whining! I can't stand it when you whine!" A child's relentless wailing, pleading, and whimpering can sound really abrasive to parents, but the negative command rarely brings it to an end. Better to describe the manner of speech the parent can accept. "If you want me to listen to what you want, speak in a cheerful tone and make your request reasonable, not emotional." This teaches the child that her own negative way of expressing her feelings, whining, won't get her what she wants. Talking, quietly, thoughtfully, and calmly is what it takes to open up conversation with you.

If you do have the need to issue a negative command to stop or prevent unsafe behavior, immediately afterwards:

- Explain why. "I told you not to cross the street in the middle because moving cars will not expect that and might not stop."
- Prescribe an alternative action instead. "Better to walk to the corner to cross, and to look both ways for traffic before you do."

A negative (stop) command blocks; a positive (start) command redirects. Prohibition limits, but instruction educates.

LYING

But what happens when your child commits the cardinal sin of communication—lying? Lying always sets up the same conflicts: fiction versus truth, evasion versus honesty, denial versus admission. It creates tension between the liar, who wants to fabricate, and the person lied to, who resents being misled. The purpose of lying is to take advantage of the other person's trust or ignorance and to create a false impression. It is normal, for example, for adolescents to lead double lives, partly known and partly not known to their parents. But substance-abusing teenagers who lie to hide their habit become truly unknown within their families. This is why all recovery programs emphasize honesty with oneself and with others.

To encourage honesty, parents need to explain to young children, and again to adolescents, how costly telling lies is to the liar. A young child will often lie for the fun of making up a story, to fabricate an image to enhance his social reputation, or to escape the consequences of wrongdoing. Here the parent can explain the importance of truth telling, "It's fun to pretend, but don't use make-believe to make me believe what isn't true. You need to tell me the truth so I can trust the stories you tell me. You need to be honest so I know that you are who you say you are. And you need to confess to what you did so we can deal with it and move on. Most important, notice how you feel when you lie to me. Not as close and comfortable as when you trust me with the truth."

With adolescents, lying becomes more frequent and complex. Adolescents tend to tell lies for the sake of doing the forbidden and not getting caught. Their social freedom is at stake. Here parents need to itemize the high costs of lying. They can start by explaining that deception is deceptively simple. To the teenager, lying seems like the easy way out, but it is not. From what I have seen in counseling over the years, lying gets teenagers into more trouble than any other behavior.

Frequent lying places them not only in a false position with others, but in an increasingly untenable position with themselves. Liars live in fear of being found out, which is why they tend to become more secretive and less communicative with parents. They become lonely and isolated in the family because they have distanced themselves to avoid giving themselves away. They feel out of control because after covering up one lie with another, they soon can't keep their stories straight. They may even become so confused that they start believing some of their own lies. Deceiving loved ones who trust them makes them feel progressively worse about themselves. Feeling that they lack the courage to tell the truth lowers their self-esteem. Finally, when their deception is discovered, they are increasingly surrounded by angry family members who feel hurt and who may no longer trust them. Now, even when they tell the truth, they are less likely to be believed. No wonder they are relieved when they are found out and have to own up to their lies. Now they can stop all this duplicity, get back on an honest footing with others, and relax in the close company of those they love. That's the lesson a lot of teenage liars learn: it's hurtful to be lied to, but it's far less hurtful than being the person who has been telling lies.

It is important for parents to confront the issue of dishonesty because in children who lie and get away with it, lying is more likely to become habitual, affecting other relationships now and later. Therefore, if you think your child lies, you should

- treat it seriously as a denial of truth and a breach of trust;
- let the child know how it feels to be lied to (you feel angry, scared, hurt, sad) so that he knows how lies emotionally impact relationships;
- ask why he felt the need to lie to you so that he identifies his motivation;
- impose some token consequence for lying to work off the offense and signify that lying is not okay;
- discuss how next time the child can choose to be honest; and
- reinstate parental trust in the expectation that henceforth truth will be told.

Parents often have a hard time with this last requirement, wanting to withhold trust until the child "earns it back." I disagree with this approach for several reasons. First, in a healthy family people trust each other to tell the truth, and by reinstating trust you are holding him to the same healthy, honest account as any other family member so that he can start choosing to tell you the truth. Second, if you don't trust your child to tell the truth, he may wonder why he should bother to be honest since he will not be believed. This doesn't mean you do not increase your vigilance. You do. You look for signs that truth is forthcoming, that his words and actions now match up, that he keeps his promises, and that he makes an effort to be more open with you. Third, by withholding trust you can drive yourself crazy with distrust, which does neither you nor your child any good. Your need to trust is as much for your sake as his. Increased vigilance in the wake of a child lying is one thing, but ongoing suspicion is another. The uncertainty creates enormous stress for you. You can't control whether he lies to you again, but you can control your determination to give him the chance to be honest, and to confront him yet again if he is not. That confrontation can include making reparation to someone whom he has misrepresented with a lie. So when he tells you that his teacher didn't assign homework when he knows she did, you explain that he has told a lie about that teacher, and that you and he will meet with her so he can confess, apologize, and figure out some way to make amends. He needs to know that lying about other people can be an offense against them. His lie made it seem as if she was not doing her job. Not only can lying misrepresent other people, it can also be an act of complicity when it covers up for friends, and a parent may choose to hold his child accountable for that.

Another form of lying that is particularly challenging involves misrepresenting misconduct as something else in order to excuse it. This type of lying occurs more commonly in adolescence than in childhood because it requires verbal sophistication. The teenager admits what he did but calls it something else to make it seem okay. Consider three examples.

- He steals something from you and when you ask him about it, he tells you he was just "borrowing" it.
- He insults you and denies any intent to hurt your feelings by saying that he was just "joking."
- He breaks a promise and blames it on absent-mindedness, saying that he "forgot."

In all three cases he is denying his responsibility and implying that you are to blame for overreacting or not understanding his true motives.

The more often he mischaracterizes his actions to feign innocence, the more you have to challenge him about it directly. "You say you were just teasing your sister about her weight, but I think calling her 'Piggy' was meant to be insulting. I would like to talk about why you wanted to hurt her feelings like that."

ATTRIBUTION ERRORS

What if both parties are expressing their feelings honestly in conflict, but one or both wrongly attribute different thoughts, feelings, and motivations to their words. *Attribution errors* are common, and they intensify conflict.

What is an attribution error? Suppose a wife disagrees with a discipline decision her husband has made, and when she tells him she would rather try another approach, he is furious. "Why are you getting so angry?" she wants to know. "All I said was that I don't think we need to ground him for an entire month." "I'm angry because you're criticizing me!" he yells. And she feels falsely accused, "How do you get from 'I disagree with you' to 'I disapprove of you'? That never even crossed my mind!" So the man ends up in a fight because he attributed meaning to his wife's comments that wasn't there instead of just discussing the discipline issue at hand.

As one psychologist put it, "The fundamental attribution error refers to a tendency to attribute other people's behavior to more dispositional causes, underestimating the importance of situational factors."[4] The parent who smiles nervously to cover up his discomfort in a disagreement with his child may end up encouraging a common attribution error. His teenage son misses the discomfort and instead reads mockery into his father's smile. "Stop laughing at me!" he shouts, "You never take me seriously!" Another psychologist concludes, "The attribution process is prone to errors and biases...and the inability to process information rationally."[5] Or, consider the teenager in family counseling trying to talk about how he feels; his father interjects, "You need to stop pitying yourself and think of us for a change!" Whereupon, the young man, furious that his father presumes to understand his feelings, explodes, "I'm *not* pitying myself! Don't tell me how I feel! I'm upset about all that's happened, and that's okay. And I *am* thinking of you, or I wouldn't be here talking to you now!" No wonder the teenager feels insulted and angry. He has been falsely accused by his father's attribution error, and he feels hurt that he does not have the benefit of his parent's true understanding. Parent/child relationships are rife with conflicts that arise when either side is presumptively misunderstood. As one writer put it, "One of the most common cognitive failures [attribution errors] is also the most pernicious in conflict situations."[6]

A psychological function of attribution, particularly in conflict, is to make up for ignorance of the other person's disposition. Three common disposition questions are:

- What is the other person *really feeling* toward me? (Emotional)
- What is that person *really thinking* about me? (Cognitive)
- What are that person's *real intentions* toward me? (Motivational)

Attributions often express not a person's best guess but project a person's worst fears, which causes him to guess wrong. *Attribution errors can intensify conflict.*

How to minimize the likelihood of false attributions and their inflammatory impact? The guideline is simply to check them out. If you are ascribing to the other person dispositions that you find hurtful, suspicious, threatening, or offensive, then, before proceeding as if your attributions are true, ask the other person these questions:

- Did I hear you say you're disappointed with me?
- Do you really mean that you don't believe in me?
- Do you really want to have less to do with me?
- Are you feeling or thinking that I'm not worth your time?

In conflict with your child, checking out the truth of your attributions and teaching your child to do the same with you can show these attributions to be false and prevent unnecessary complications. When the nine-year-old becomes furious when his mother tells him to stop making fun of his younger sibling's proud creation, what really grieves the older boy is his belief that this "just shows" that his mother loves the younger child more. A neutral response from her helps reassure him: "I don't want that kind of teasing going on, period. If he were teasing you that way, I would be correcting him. I love you both too much to let that kind of behavior go on in this family."

Attribution errors are misperceptions that can inflict hurt, offend, cause anxiety, and complicate conflict unnecessarily, and it's important to both recognize when you are bringing your own misperceptions into conflict and to challenge this when the other party is doing it to you. As a psychologist who specializes in the study of conflict writes, "Clarifying perceptions is an essential skill if we are to deal with conflict effectively. Just as unclear mirrors and windows can distort reality, so it is that unclarified perceptions about the conflict, about ourselves, and about our conflict partners can distort and obstruct the process of conflict resolution."[7]

THREE IDEAS ABOUT *COMMUNICATION* AND *CONFLICT* TO CARRY FORWARD

- By providing two opposing ways to consider the same issue, conflict creates opportunity for parent and child to learn more about each other, including the differences between them.
- Conflict between parent and child is most effectively conducted by avoiding extreme, evaluative, and abstract language and by using words and phrases that are moderate, objective, and operational.
- When parent or child is concerned about the other's disposition (thoughts, feelings, or intent) in conflict, before responding to what is imagined, it is best to check out one's attribution.

4

INTOLERANCE AND CONFLICT

No one is universally accepting of all human variation, and thus bias and intolerance play a role in many family conflicts. This is particularly true when children challenge or stray outside of the approved family framework—misbehaving, experimenting, and differentiating as they grow. Parents communicate bias when they criticize a child's conduct. They communicate intolerance when they set limits about what they will not allow. And when a child becomes biased against herself with significant dislike, internal conflict can beget conflict with others.

A FAMILY SYSTEM IS A VALUE SYSTEM

Every family develops its own value system, that is, rules and standards based on core beliefs and traditional behaviors that parents consider normal, right, and wise. Parents pass these values to their children through example and instruction. There is no such thing as a value-free family system because there are no value-free parents. One job of parenting is to pass on values, guiding the next generation to ethical living; another is to monitor how closely children adhere to the principles they are taught.

All parents express *bias* based on their personal values and communicate intolerance to prevent those values from being breached. "That's enough!" declares the parent to the teenager when the conversation seems too vulgar, the music too grating, the poster too graphic, the slang too crude, the dress too suggestive, or the entertainment too violent. This parental bias and intolerance conflicts with adolescent interests, and the teenager accuses parents of prejudice against his generation's beliefs and values. In this way, intergenerational disagreements unfold.

How could raising a child be otherwise? Anchored in their own social and cultural background, all parents are biased by the values they were taught as children. The mother declares, "My parents believed a child should perform well in school to reflect well on the family, and I believe that too." At some point, all parents are intolerant of influences that they consider unacceptable, like the father who decrees, "I will not permit that kind of Internet content in our home!" All parents have standards for their children, and all parents set rules.

CONFLICTS OVER LEARNING

Although most parents would agree that trial, error, and recovery describe the learning curve of growing up, they can have a hard time accepting this principle with their own children. Parents who are tired or stressed may become critical of a child's uneven progress, or they may become critical because of their own exacting natures. Such parents may believe that learning should be easy, and are thus intolerant of a child's repeated mistakes. Conflicts can occur when she does not seem to try hard enough or if her learning seems too slow. The restive parent may say, "You're not paying attention!" "Why don't you do it right the first time?" "How long is this going to take?" "You made that mistake before!" "How many times do I have to show you?" The child may respond with accusations of her own, "Well, you're no help!" "You just make it harder!" "I can't do this when you get angry!" "All you do is criticize!" "I give up!" *When intolerant parents engage in conflict with a child over learning, they contribute to the child's unwillingness to learn.*

Why would parents have such insensitivity to a child's trial-and-error learning? One of the most common reasons is *instructional amnesia.* Whether tutoring an elementary school-age child on long division or teaching a teenager to drive, most parents have forgotten their own mistake-strewn efforts to master these skills. Over years of practice, the skills involved in doing simple math problems or driving become automatic to the parent, who therefore assumes that these complex proficiencies should be simple for the child to learn. A father might think, "Multiplying rows of numbers is so easy. Why doesn't my eight-year-old get it?" A mother may wonder, "Why is my daughter having so much difficulty just parking a car?" Now the stage is set for conflict between the child who is struggling to learn and the parent whose tolerance for his slow pace is running down.

It is incumbent upon parents to try to avoid these conflicts because they may have a negative impact on the child's ability and motivation to learn. The most damaging part of instructional amnesia is when parents forget that while education builds self-esteem, learning also *requires* self-esteem because learning is always *risky* to do.

To learn something new, the child must undertake five risks.

- Declare ignorance. "I don't know how!"
- Make mistakes. "I may mess up!"
- Feel stupid. "I am so slow!"
- Look foolish. "This will be embarrassing!"
- Be evaluated. "Suppose I fail?"

These risks are inherent in the learning process for people of any age—from the child learning to play a new game to the adult learning to use a computer. When a child puts her capacity to the test, her self-esteem depends on how the instructor treats the learning process. When the teachers are her parents, their response can make all the difference between opening the child up to learning as a positive challenge or turning her off to it and making it a cause for conflict. Simply put, parents can *encourage learning* if they are

- affirming of ignorance: *All learning starts with admitting what we do not know*;
- patient with mistakes: *Getting it wrong is how you learn to get it right*;
- appreciative of feeling stupid: *You're not being slow; you're learning at your own rate*;

- respectful of looking foolish: *Letting others see you struggle to learn is brave*; and
- supportive in evaluation: *Now you know more than you did before!*

This kind of support helps the child to feel confident about taking risks, because the parents have made learning feel safe and comfortable and the rewards for making an effort are high.

However, parents can *discourage learning* if they are

- irritable about ignorance: *I can't believe you don't know that*;
- impatient with mistakes: *You're not even trying*;
- critical of apparent stupidity: *What's the matter with you?*
- derisive about appearances of foolishness: *What will other people think!* or
- harshly evaluative: *You'll never get it right!*

Parental bias and intolerance make learning feel risky, and reluctance to learn in childhood can become a disability later in life. The adult who still lives in fear of criticism or failure may be inclined to shy away from challenges because it feels safer not to try.

If you ever find yourself becoming impatient, frustrated, irritated, critical, sarcastic, or angry, step out of the instructional role. Do not re-engage until you can do so in a supportive way. Feelings of frustration or irritability when your child makes mistakes are a sign that you may be allowing bias and intolerance to impede this vital process. Criticizing a child for not catching on fast enough can undermine his confidence and make him unwilling to take the necessary risks of learning. Learning is behavioral change—acquiring skills or knowledge one did not possess before. And like any behavior change, it usually takes time to put it securely in place. Trial and error are part of the practice that is required, moving two steps forward and one step back through progress and regress until consistency of action or understanding is finally accomplished. That's when mastery is achieved. Parents must be patient with this process as their child grows. The toddler is finally toilet trained, but not without some accidents along the way.

If an older child ridicules a younger child's efforts to learn something new, make sure the older child is aware of the house rules: "When someone is making an effort to learn something new in this family, we should be supportive instead of critical." In addition, parents need to set a good example. A parent who tries to assemble a new household device and has difficulty following the directions may explode in frustration: "What's the matter with this thing? What's the matter with me? The heck with it! I just give up!" The message to the child is "When understanding gets frustrating, curse the task, criticize yourself, and stop trying to learn."

DEALING WITH SOCIAL DIFFERENCES

Beginning between the ages of nine and thirteen and not ending until the early to mid-twenties, adolescence changes a young person's life. In childhood, his primary self-identification and social affiliation are with his family and parents. In adolescence, his focus increasingly becomes the peer group.

As the young person begins the process of emotionally separating from family, parents, who were once the child's in-group, become the adolescent's out-group. What do these terms mean? According to one psychologist who has extensively studied the dynamics of intergroup bias and conflict, "the fact that individuals value, favor, and conform to their own memberships groups (in-groups) over groups to which they do not belong (out-groups) is among the most well-established phenomena in social psychology."[1] The price of forsaking the family in-group is often a loss of closeness with parents. The teenager may feel jealous of her younger siblings, who are still firmly anchored in parental approval and who seem to enjoy a degree of favor that the teenager has given up.

Establishing his new in-group demonstrates independence, provides like-minded support and companionship, and creates a personal and social identity different from that of childhood and family. The price of membership in a new in-group, however, can be steep. Peer-group membership can become restrictive when an adolescent sacrifices personal freedom in exchange for social standing. In extreme cases the message from peers is something like, If you want to be one of us,

- believe as we do,
- behave as we do,
- be loyal to us,

- don't betray us,
- don't like others as well as you like us, and
- don't do better than us.

Conform, fit in, follow along, and be different in the same way we are: these are the informal requirements for being part of the group. It is no wonder that parents feel like outsiders, suddenly peripheral to the adolescent's life. Parents can feel as if they are fighting for *family* influence against the *foreign* influence of their teenager's newfound friends, and it can be difficult for parents to resist expressing bias and intolerance. As for the young person, the more she identifies and affiliates with peers, the more separate from parents she usually feels. In this way, the social independence of adolescence causes the parents and young person to grow apart, for which each often blames the other. In counseling, when I see each party faulting the other in these intergenerational conflicts, it reminds me of a quote from T. S. Eliot's play *Family Reunion*: "In a world of fugitives the person taking the opposite direction will appear to run away."[2] When you feel like blaming your adolescent for being more distant, it can be helpful to remember that from the teenager's point of view, you have become more distant, too. And, as Eliot points out, it is easier to attribute the cause for estrangement to others than to ourselves. "You never talk to me!" accuses the parent. "You never listen to me!" complains the teenager. In counseling, the parent may finally admit that she has become less tolerant of her teenager's behavior, but she may still blame their conflicts on the teenager's inadequate communication skills. In turn, the teenager may admit to being less communicative but blame the problem on the parent's closed-mindedness. To break through this logjam, the teenager should be encouraged to express how she would like to be better understood, and parents should explain their desire to better understand.

A teenager's new social life can cause concern for parents about the company he keeps. They do not want their child to have unruly friends or running with the "wrong crowd" to lead him to reject their values. Out of fear, they may judge his potential companions by their family's social or economic standing or by personal appearance, particularly style of dress. In extreme cases, bias can result in *prejudice* based on stereotyping, as when parents declare, "Kids who dress that way are just headed for trouble." Intolerance can lead to *discrimination*, as when parents command, "You can't go out with people who look like that or have them over to our house." Unwilling to give up his new in-group, the teenager fights back, "My friends are up to me, not to you!"

Not only does the young person feel criticized when his parents reject his friends, but he feels it is unfair for his parents to condemn out of hand people whom they may not know or only barely know. Parents are really victims of their own stereotyping when they frighten themselves with such thoughts as "My child's new friends are nothing but troublemakers."

Adolescents will generally defend their right to choose their own friends. Parents who try to restrict this social independence often alienate their teenager. Parents are usually better served by getting to know his friends because

- personal acquaintance reduces the ignorance on which stereotypes depend,
- acceptance of his friends communicates acceptance of him, and
- relating to his friends can give parents a measure of influence.

Why, parents might ask, should we allow friends of our child whom we do not like or trust into our home? The response should be the ancient advice: Always keep your enemies close. This tactic may lead to the discovery that they are not enemies after all.

Once parents have accepted the new in-group, they can better communicate their concerns, "We want you to have fun with your friends. What we don't want is for you to act with these companions, or with anybody else, in ways that you know we disapprove of or believe to be unsafe. So enjoy your friends, but please respect our wishes." Should parents ever have the need, for safety's sake, to limit the association, they can do so, not by criticizing the teenager's friends, but by disagreeing with his choice of behavior when in their company. "We can't have you going out and accepting rides with friends who drink and drive." If he is unable to resist joining in unsafe behavior, parents may have to limit his social interactions to those that take place in the home. It is important for parents to hold the teenager responsible for his conduct with friends rather than blaming it on the coercive nature of the group.

DEALING WITH DEVELOPMENTAL DIFFERENCES

Developmental differentiation refers to the adolescent's shift of identity away from the childhood self. Adolescent differentiation increases diversity of self-expression and self-definition in the young person. Parents' ability to accept and tolerate these differences in their teenager influences the frequency and intensity of the conflicts between them. As one psychologist notes, "[T]hese differences often lead to conflict.... In dealing with [these] conflicts, the point is not to remove the differences but to use the differences to (1) clarify our understanding of each other and the relationship, (2) consider ideas and possibilities we may not have thought about, and (3) see if there are aspects of the relationship on which we can build effectively to improve the relationship."[3]

It can be useful for parents to explain the limits of their acceptance and tolerance to the teenager, because *acceptance does not necessarily mean agreement.* You can say, "We accept your enthusiasm for violent entertainment even though we don't share it." Agreeing to disagree is one way to respectfully resolve value differences. And tolerance does not necessarily mean granting total permission. You can say, "We know we must get used to you having more freedom now that you're a teenager, but that doesn't mean there are no rules." One way to resolve differences over freedom is to dispense permission in proportion to responsibility assumed. Freedom must be earned.

Parents also need to make a clear separation between their *honest dislike* and their *abiding love* in order to reduce the child's vulnerability for emotional injury when in conflict with them. She needs to feel secure that it is her conduct that is at issue for parents, not their caring for her. She should not equate parental disapproval or disagreement with any loss of love. In conflict with them, she needs to be confident that "they really don't like what I did, but they love me as much as ever."

The most important thing is to explain to your teenager that it is natural at this age for differences to come between you. Try saying something like, "I want you to understand that no differences between us can ever drive us apart. Only how we handle our differences can do that. Like if we were to decide that a dispute was grounds for not talking to each other." The dividing issue is like the border between two countries; it connects them through common ground. Fighting about chores reflects our common concern over housework. Fighting about curfew reflects our common concern about socializing. Fighting about clothes reflects our common concern about appearance. "Whatever divides us also connects us. Every time we disagree it means we have something important *in common* to talk about." Unfortunately, there are parents who cannot see connection when a difference with their teenager arises; they can only see division.

Parents who are biased to the point of rigidity and unwilling to look beyond their own point of view are at a disadvantage in dealing with the developmental differences that arise during adolescence. They see only either/or choices—*my* way or *your* way. They *talk at* her but they do not *listen to* her. They care about control, not communication.

Parental absolutes allow no discussion of alternatives or of compromises. "There will be no body piercing, tattoos, dyed hair, or wearing torn clothes to school while you live in our house!" No wonder adolescents defensively resort to absolutes in response. But parents can remain faithful to their convictions without stating them as absolutes. For example, they might explain to their daughter that just because they disagree with her fashion choices, it doesn't mean they refuse to discuss her point of view. "Just because we won't allow something you want, doesn't mean we don't want to understand it." When agreement cannot be reached, understanding may have to do.

This concept should be applied to *personal tastes and interests,* which increasingly serve to differentiate the adolescent from the parent. Contesting superficial preferences such as taste in music, entertainment, food, dress, recreation, appearance, consumer products, or even celebrities can create deep intergenerational divides. The best advice for parents who abhor their adolescent's latest fascination with popular culture is to not try to change his taste, but to enlist his help in trying to understand it. For example, a fifteen-year-old son announces how he thinks fight clubs are "cool," while his parents see them as nothing more than opportunities for boys to give or get hurt. By separating interest from action, the parents make an effective response. "We respect the manly value you place on this activity now that you have explained it to us. What we want you to respect is our desire that you do not actually participate, as bystander or fighter, in what we now understand has some popular appeal."

ADOLESCENCE EQUALS THE LOSS OF CHILDHOOD

The "loss" of the adored and adoring child makes adjusting to the adolescent difficult for many parents. Gone is the child as best buddy and constant companion who enjoyed nothing so much as to be by the parent's side. Gone is the child who idealized the parent who basked in being so admired. Gone is the child who regularly strove to please the parent. Gone are the harmony they shared and the ease of getting along. Gone is the golden time when just being together, it didn't matter doing what, was fun. Now peers are the adolescent's preferred companions. Now displeasing the parent more often seems the order of the day. Now arguing is a common occurrence. Now being together feels distant, awkward, and strained. All of these changes are *necessary losses,* and better to honor them with grief than turn to *grievance.* It is important not to lash out in anger with such remarks as "You used to be such a great kid; what happened to you?" This undermines her newly forming sense of self and can make her feel guilty for growing up.

Because parents invest so much in a child, and because they must become less salient in order for her to change during adolescence, the healthy outcome of growing up is a harsh reality. In the words of one wise writer, this reality is that "children always mean more to parents than parents mean to children."[4] Parents should be careful not to take offence when the differentiating adolescent becomes more critical of them. Adolescence is all about the search for an independent and authentic grown-up identity. This search is conducted by differentiating on two fronts—from how the teenager defined himself in childhood and from his current perception of his parents. The adolescent subjects his parents to a process of *contrast and comparison*, which is inevitably followed by some degree of *criticism* based on his "findings." Parents should not take it personally, particularly when the criticism is stated not simply as disagreement but as *dislike*. "What I can't stand about you is..." (Your teenager can complete the sentence.) Deciding to dislike a quality, attitude, or behavior in his parents helps the teenager see himself as a different and sometimes better kind of person. For example, "My parents only care about appearance and reputation. I don't care about those things; I think who a person is on the inside is what's important." Although leveled at parents, this kind of comment is really about the teenager. His parents become his point of reference, which he modifies in order to redefine himself. And parents should not conclude that this rejection of some aspect of them means that they are not valued, do not matter, and are not loved. There is no need to feel defensive during this normal and necessary process of contrast, comparison, and criticism. This expression of dislike is part of adolescent differentiation, and it is not something to fight about. It is to be expected and accepted.

The adolescent needs to differentiate from the child she was, from her former role in the family, from the parents that she used to emulate, and from the person her parents still sometimes want her to be. When you approach her in the old spirit of childish play, she may protest: "Don't talk to me that way. I'm not your little girl anymore!"

This challenging transition affects family communication. As most parents of teenagers will testify, living with a sixteen-year-old is very different from living with her when she was a child. The eight-year-old wanted to be like her parents, who found communication with her relatively easy. This sense of closeness encouraged compatibility and comfort, knowledge and familiarity, predictability and trust, agreement and harmony. Contrast this with the incompatibility and discomfort, ignorance and anxiety, unpredictability and distrust, and disagreement and conflict parents often experience with the teenager. As researchers have described, "Parent-adolescent conflict[s] ... [are] predominantly verbal disputes concerning specific issues; these conflicts are regarded as a natural developmental phenomenon that results when young adolescents begin to individuate from the nuclear family."[5] *For many parents, attachment to the memory of the beloved child contributes to a bias against the teenager and anger at how different their relationship with her is becoming.*

ADOLESCENCE EQUALS DIFFERENTIATION

Adolescent differentiation from parents occurs on four major levels:

- *Character differences.* These are nonchosen dimensions of being, such as physical stature, psychological temperament, and personality traits. The child who used to literally look up to her parents is now taller than her mother; the child who used to be childlike now seems adult; the child who was once always cheerful is now moody; and the child who used to be outgoing has become introverted.
- *Value differences.* These are beliefs about right and wrong, about what is desirable and undesirable, appropriate and inappropriate, or correct and incorrect. These convictions are culturally acquired and transmitted from parent to child more through osmosis than through formal instruction. The child who used to see the world through the traditional lens of parental perspective becomes the adolescent who identifies with the alternative values of peers, youth icons, and popular culture.
- *Habit differences.* These are patterns of behavior that have been practiced over time. The child who was "early to bed and early to rise" becomes the nocturnal adolescent who is later to bed and harder to wake for school. The child who used to respond promptly to parental requests now usually stalls and (in parental parlance) "takes forever" to get things done.
- *Want differences.* These are conscious desires to be, do, or have something or not. Of the four levels, want differences are the most amenable to change because they are the most subject to conscious choice. The child who chose to be content to operate within the family circle becomes the adolescent who is restless and wants to be out in the company of friends. Or the one who chose to ignore his appearance now wants to wear the latest fashion.

Attached as they still are to the memory of their darling and delightful child, parents can be critical of their teenagers on all four levels of adolescent change.

- Taking issue with a character difference, a parent complains: "Why don't you stop moping around and acting so irritable?" To which the teenager, who is often at the mercy of his moods, replies: "Why don't you stop picking on me when I'm feeling down!"
- Taking issue with a value difference, a parent complains: "You call that music? I call it noise! Turn it off!" To which the teenager, for whom the angry lyrics and blasting sound provide a satisfying outlet for his growing discontent, replies: "The music you like has *nothing* to say. It's *boring*!"
- Taking issue with a habit difference, a parent complains: "You'd be less tired and grumpy in the morning if you got a normal good night's sleep!" To which the teenager, for whom a late night is another avenue for independence, replies: "I'm too old to go to bed that early!"
- Taking issue with a want difference, a parent complains: "You don't need new clothes when you have a whole closet full of them!" To which the teenager, who is concerned with his social image, replies: "I'm not going to school to be laughed at for wearing something that's out of style!"

What parents sometimes underestimate is how the confidence of childhood is often subverted by the psychological discomfort and social alterations of adolescence, particularly when they coincide with the physiological changes of puberty. The young person entering puberty begins to develop enormous self-consciousness and insecurity, which frequently lead to *self-rejection,* in other words, bias toward and intolerance of herself. For the majority of young people, even though the changes of sexual maturity are a sign of growing up, puberty feels like a change for the worse. They are not in control of their bodies and have significant concerns about how they are going to turn out. At an age when many young boys and girls "can't stand" their personal appearance, readily believe that "nobody" likes them, and sometimes feel "worthless," expressions of parental bias in the form of criticism or humorous put-downs can really sting. At an age when fashion (fitting in) and popularity (social status) support fragile self-esteem, parental intolerance of her tastes in clothes or friends can devastate a young person, who needs to identify and be with her peers.

If parents really want to avoid unnecessary conflict, it behooves them to be nonjudgmental. Remember that *she is likely to be in conflict with herself—the positive qualities she wishes she had being constantly arrayed against the negative qualities she believes she has.* When she's most down on herself is when she's usually most up for a fight with you.

Instead of cooperating in conflict, parents can practice two strategies for turning it into communication, by

- treating the teen as an informant not an opponent, and learning to *bridge* differences and not to battle them; and
- recognizing and respecting what they cannot change about the teen, and committing to resolve all conflicts below *the rejection line.*

THE REJECTION LINE

It helps if parents communicate to children that differences between family members are never to be treated as a problem, but should be accepted as part of our human reality. It can also help if parents make a distinction between differences in character, values, and habits, which are all strongly set, and differences in wants, which are much more changeable. The first three tend to be intransigent: temperament and personality are endowed and therefore not easily altered; tastes and convictions are deeply instilled and therefore often not questioned; and rituals and routines become second nature. That leaves want differences as the most open to discussion, negotiation, and modification.

The rejection line, as I call it, separates the first three levels of differences from the fourth. When you criticize or tell someone to change an intractable dimension of themselves like their character, value, or habits, they tend to feel offended because you are rejecting something fundamental about them that they cannot, at least not easily, change. You are communicating that they are not acceptable in your eyes. This often leads to demand/defend conflicts. Consider these typical scenarios.

- On the character level, the twelve-year-old may be suffering through the hormonal effects of puberty. Tired of her mood swings, her parents *demand,* "Stop acting so emotional, you're impossible to live with!" She *defends* her unpredictable intensity: "That's just the way I am. I'm tired of you criticizing me all the time!"

- On a value level, the teenager may be undergoing a countercultural change, blasting music on his bedroom stereo or dressing to identify with the disaffected peers who are now his primary in-group. His disapproving parents *demand,* "We don't want you hanging around with those people anymore!" He *defends* his social choice: "I can choose my own friends! Who I hang out with is none of your business!"
- On a habit level, the teenager may be hooked on the computer, spending hours in front of it, "talking" to friends but ignoring family. Her worried parents *demand,* "You don't need to spend all your time instant messaging!" She *defends* the importance of this communication: "I need to keep up with what's going on!"

Engaging in conflicts over aspects of her normal differentiation process invites your teenager to defend her identity, preferences, and lifestyle changes. But don't be fooled. Your criticism also makes her feel rejected and undermines her fragile self-esteem. It is more effective to *translate your objections into things that you want and negotiate for them below the rejection line.*

- When addressing the emotional outbursts often characteristic of puberty, parents can say, "It's okay. It's normal for you to feel more emotional intensity when you are going through puberty. What we want is to work out ways to express these important feelings that also work for us. We would like to be sensitive and supportive."
- Addressing countercultural values and antipathy to family tradition, parents could say, "We know this is a time for you to have friends with different beliefs. What we want is for you to have those friends and for us to know them in a way that also works for us."
- Addressing changes in habits that come with wanting to act older, parents could say, "We know that talking to your friends on the computer is important to you. We want to allow you that freedom, but at the same time for you to communicate to us so we also feel that we are adequately in touch with you."

Conflicts with adolescents over intractable differences of character, value, or habits are best dealt with through acceptance and translation.

This means parents *accept* the offending issue of character, value, or habit and then *translate* their objection into what they want to have happen, or want not to have happen, discussing and resolving the matter *below the rejection line where nobody feels attacked, criticized, or blamed.*

BRIDGING DIFFERENCES—THE GENERATION GAP

The cultural forces that shaped parents during childhood are very different from those that shape teenagers today. Teenagers feel frustrated by their parents' limited comprehension of the contemporary world, while ignorance of adolescent culture breeds parental anxiety and distrust. Parents who are suspicious of trends are prone to criticize or try to suppress those they find strange or unwelcome. Songwriter Bob Dylan voiced the universal youthful response to parental censure when he sang, "Don't criticize what you can't understand."[6]

Criticism is, of course, easier than understanding, but it can shut down communication at a time when parents need to know what is going on in their teenager's life. They need an expert guide to her world—and that teacher can be their teenager if they are honestly curious and interested in listening and learning. Differences don't have to be barriers to the relationship, or battle points—they can be bridges to understanding. You can turn your teenager from an opponent into an informant by making the following bridging requests:

- Can you help me understand?
- Tell me more about…
- Explain to me.
- Share with me.
- Show me.
- Take me along.
- Tell me what I am missing or not getting.

When bridging requests are made, parent and teenager temporarily reverse roles. Now the adolescent is the person with instructional power and the parent is the student. Not only is this reversal informative for the parent, it validates the teenager and raises his self-esteem to know that his parents respect his opinions and knowledge. Consider the mother who is put off by her rebellious fourteen-year-old's open admiration of the young urban outlaws celebrated in current music and movies, who brazenly defy authority, break laws, and engage in violence. She fears that what he hears and sees will encourage him to act in similar ways. It is difficult to understand her son's attraction to these cultural models, since they are not part of her cultural experience. However, rather than allowing bias to cause her to become critical and intolerance to cause her to forbid continued exposure, she bridges this difference in values by asking her son to explain the appeal of these models. So they listen to some music and watch some movies together. He explains that what speaks to him is not the criminality and brutality, but rather the social freedom of these figures who are unafraid of authority and law, who dare to break the normal bounds of emotional, social, and physical restraint, who are excited by the risks they take. Because she talked openly with him about their appeal, the mother also better understands that his admiration of outlaws does not mean he intends to become one. The parent's genuine curiosity bridged this difference in values. The parent has learned that at an age when the freedom to grow feels so important and restrictions of that freedom are so frustrating, these youthful icons have enormous symbolic appeal. Most important, she has allowed herself to be taught about a very different adolescent world than she grew up in, and she is wiser for her son's instruction.[7]

Children will continue to differentiate from their former selves as well as from you throughout their adult lives, particularly when they find a partner. So it is important to learn the art of bridging differences while they are still in your care, or later conflict or estrangement may follow. The key to bridging is, as one writer suggests, transforming "judgment to curiosity.... [Doing this] a couple of things happen. First, we can admit to ourselves, however reluctantly, that the other person has their own story about the conflict.... Second, we might actually learn something.... The other person might provide information that dramatically changes our perspective in the situation. And by remaining curious we can understand their motivation and uncover their interests and needs."[8]

A powerful example is the gender difference between father and teenage daughter. The silent conflict of estrangement can easily trouble their relationship when it is not bridged. This failure occurs when a father's sexual bias prevents him from accepting his teenager's growth into young womanhood and creates a barrier between them. He discredits his daughter's way because it is different from the male way he knows. In consequence, the young woman can feel discounted or even dismissed by her father who remains disconnected except to question and correct her. Now the daughter may interpret her father's inability to relate as a criticism of her, as a sign that she is not a person worth taking seriously. Should she agree with this sad conclusion, she will diminish her own self esteem.[9] If as a dad you ever feel estranged from your adolescent daughter, make an effort to bridge the gender gap. There is a world of young womanly experience that a father should try to understand.

EXTREME DIFFERENTIATION CONFLICTS

The adolescent differences that are most difficult to bridge are those that arise when your child feels so attached to you that adolescent separation requires a dramatic statement of contrast. *Differentiation to the extreme* can create a very intense adolescent passage. For example, parents who are teachers have an adolescent who starts to fail at school and act as if he doesn't care about academic achievement. Or the lawyer who prosecutes wrongdoers has a teenager who begins to run with lawbreaking peers. The father who hates loud music has a daughter who listens to heavy metal. The parent who is known for advocating a certain social cause has a teenager whose behavior flouts that cause in public. In these very difficult situations, criticism and prohibition, although tempting for parents, usually intensifies the opposition because the teenager will fight to defend his or her emerging individual and independent self.

The most effective response is to attempt to bridge the differences so communication is not lost. For example, the teacher-parent asks the academically disaffected teenager: "Could you tell me why you are so down on education? I know we see it differently, and although we intend to keep after you about getting the work done, I would really like to understand why school is so hard and unrewarding for you right now. I don't want to change your mind; I just want to listen to what you have to say."

To maintain perspective it helps to remember that developmental differences of a high-contrast kind are usually of a *trial* rather than a *terminal* nature. Once the teenager establishes the emotional distance from his parents that he needs and is more secure in his own identity, he will often return to his parents' values. The fourteen-year-old who insists that he's not going to college because "there is nothing practical you can do with it" ends up not just going to college, but getting a masters degree. Why? Not because his teacher-parents want him to, but because he is older and no longer blinded by his need to dramatically reject everything they represent. He decided for himself that he wanted an education. Until this happens, parents need to keep bridging differences, treating each conflict as an opportunity for more communication, treating conflict for what it truly can be—a way to build intimacy.

CONFLICT AS INTIMACY BUILDING

Intimacy is the state of being close to another person; it's a process of coming to know another person and becoming better known by that person, of exchanging personal information of two kinds—what they have in common and the differences that set them apart. In most cases, people find it easier to share what they have in common because it favors harmony and agreement. This is why parents tend to feel closer to a child who enjoys being like them, than to an adolescent who wants to be different from them. Differences can lead to disagreement and conflict. To avoid conflict, or to treat conflict only as a contest for control, reduces the deeper knowing that honoring diversity and bridging differences can create. The dominant parent who declares (and the submissive teenager who agrees) that "we always get along and never have any conflict" is sacrificing intimacy. The daughter declines to share important information about herself, and the father is oblivious. He doesn't get to understand her and she doesn't get to be understood. How sad! This is what happens, however, when significant differences (at least on the adolescent's side) have not been recognized, raised, openly discussed, or resolved. Peace at all costs in family relationships is a bad bargain because of the cost: intimacy is lost.

TRUE INCOMPATIBILITIES

Sometimes there are real incompatibilities between parents and their children, simple mismatches of temperament, personality, or style that lead to conflict for which no one is to blame. The soft-spoken parent who hates loud talking because she grew up in a raucous household chides her young son: "Your shrill tone of voice when you get excited really rubs me the wrong way." But what is the boy supposed to do? Not get excited? As one psychologist has observed, "Personality and temperamental mismatches between parent and child can be a source of conflict, disappointment, and heartache for both. They can also lead to long-term alienation between parents and their child."[10] In counseling a parent and child together, I try to help them cope with true incompatibilities by encouraging them to use their sense of humor, because humor can facilitate acceptance. I tell them that life is truly funny the way it continually places people in relationships, even family relationships, where fundamental mismatches in tastes and temperaments occur. I suggest that it is far better for all concerned to learn to laugh at these incompatibilities than to be offended by them. "So," one father smiled, "I guess there's nothing wrong with either of us, nothing we need to fight about. We're just very different when it comes to getting things done, and we just need to get used to that. I want to push myself hard, and you like to stay as relaxed as you can be." His smiling teenage daughter agreed.

STEPFAMILY DIFFERENCES

Although such mismatches can occur in any family, they are most sharply illuminated in *stepfamilies*, where incompatibilities are often put to the hardest test. Stepfamily relationships are complicated in ways that original family relationships are not. Consider how dynamics in the two settings typically contrast.

- In the original family, there is acceptance of individual differences among members because of their historical experience with each other and because commitment and love create tolerance. This is not the case in step families. One parent has adjusted to his children's lax table manners, while the stepparent thinks reaching across the table for food is the height of rudeness and won't stand for it.
- In the original family, there is more genetic similarity and shared family culture and tradition. This is not the case in stepfamilies, where the stepparent may want to institute holiday observances that feel foreign and unwelcome to the stepchildren who, for example, are used to celebrating Christmas the morning of, not the night before.
- In the original family, children tend not to compete with one adult for time and primacy with the other adult. This is not so in stepfamilies, where stepchild and stepparent can feel like rivals for the other adult's attention at the end of the day.
- In the original family, the governing authority of parents was accepted by children from birth. This is not so in stepfamilies, where, as far as stepchildren are concerned, a new adult with no historical family standing has no right to make or enforce rules.
- In the original family, there were no loyalty conflicts complicating parent/child relationships. This is not so in stepfamilies, where stepchildren can feel deeply ambivalent toward a stepparent out of loyalty to their absent biological parent. Or, when both adults bring children into the remarriage, loyalty can cause or appear to cause them to favor their own children, creating resentment.

Stepfamilies experience a host of complicated issues that original families are spared. Stepfamily relationships increase diversity (a pool of human differences) in a family at the same time that people in those relationships have not had time to get used to each other, to grow fond of each other, or to learn how to tolerate and resolve their differences.

A parent and stepparent marry intentionally for love, but the stepparent and stepchild are *accidentally married* in the bargain, forced into a familial affiliation not based on love. Mismatches abound as stepparent and stepchild find themselves in what I call *no-fault collisions* with each other, clashes of incompatibilities for which no one is to blame.[11] The adults' new match creates many *mis*matches between stepparent and stepchildren. The new union may be a minefield of incompatibilities waiting to explode.

If original families have difficulty navigating differences, the increased family diversity in stepfamilies is even more challenging, particularly during adolescence. In stepfamilies, these differences can become so powerfully divisive that conflict can never be resolved, contributing to the extremely high divorce rate for second marriages. The rate of divorce for remarriages without children is higher than for first marriages, whereas the rate of divorce in remarriages with stepchildren is highest of all (about 75%), a fact that has been partly attributed to the stress of step relationships.

Here are some of the incompatibility problems that accidental marriage can create.

- On the level of *character*, the stepparent is extremely deliberate, while the stepchild is extremely impulsive.
- On the level of *values*, the stepparent believes in planning ahead and considering consequences and objectives, while the stepchild believes in being spontaneous.
- On the level of *habits*, the stepparent is wed to routines, while the stepchild loves the excitement of the new.
- On the level of *wants*, the stepparent likes order, while the stepchild is comfortable with disarray.

In frustration, the stepparent accuses the stepchild of being a "slob" and the stepchild accuses the stepparent of being a "neat freak." Such inflammatory, pejorative labels arouse angry and hurt feelings. Repeated attacks *above the rejection line* will cause damage, grievance, and opposition resulting from bias against and intolerance of differences that are not very susceptible to change.

A *non*inflammatory exchange in this situation would be focused on offending behaviors—what the stepchild is specifically doing or not doing that causes the stepparent to use the term slob, and what the stepparent is specifically doing or not doing that causes the stepchild to use the term neat freak. The behavioral changes that each party wants could be discussed below the rejection line to see what changes might be negotiated and what diversity must simply be accepted. Whether in an original family or an accidental marriage, incompatibilities that cannot be bridged or resolved below the rejection line must be *accommodated*. Individuals must learn to work around, ignore, or put up with each other's differences. To criticize or fight what you cannot change will only be frustrating for you, painful to the other person, and destructive of your relationship.

One danger of taking issue with any incompatible difference is making it seem greater than it really is. *Reductionist thinking* can do a lot of damage, as when the stepchild sees the stepparent as nothing *but* unreasonable or the stepparent sees the stepchild as nothing *but* uncooperative. Now perspective has been lost. It is better for the adult to lead the way toward understanding that *any difference between us is a small piece of a relationship that is made up of other parts that are working together well.*

HOW BIAS CREATES CONFLICT

All problems result from bias, which springs from intolerance and being judgmental and sets up a dichotomy: how things are versus how we would like them to be.

- The way I am is not the way I want to be. *I don't like how I look.*
- The way you are is not the way I want you to be. *I don't like how you've become so critical of me.*
- The way our relationship works is not the way I want it to. *I don't like that we argue all the time.*
- How life is going is not how I how I want it to be. *I don't like how this situation is shaping up.*

When someone says they have a problem with themselves, with other people, or with their circumstances based on a judgment they have made or a bias they hold, they are in a *declared state of unresolved conflict*. From this state of irresolution, a dissatisfaction develops that can range all the way from mild discomfort to major unhappiness. These feelings provide the motivation to solve the problem, which can only be done in one of three ways:

- by changing the way things are to the way we'd like them to be,
- by changing what we want so that we can accept the way things are, or
- by changing some of what we want and some of the way things are to reach a compromise we can live with.

All problem solving is an exercise in conflict resolution. The stocky fifteen-year-old who tearfully tells her parents that she hates her appearance angrily rejects their reassurance that she looks fine: "You only say that because you love me!" To help her solve this problem, her parents can help articulate three choices.

1. Through diet and exercise, she can try to change the way she is (heavyset) to what she wants to be (thinner).
2. By understanding how her body is maturing, she can try to accept how she currently is.
3. By mixing an effort to change with self-acceptance, she can reach a compromise (thinner, but not rail thin).

The daughter's state of irresolution will cause a certain amount of free-floating dissatisfaction until and unless she is able to resolve this problem. Such self-dissatisfaction is likely to come out as irritation with others, provoking her younger sibling to complain: "Why do you have to be in such a bad mood all the time? You're always getting upset. And you're mean!" When the younger sibling stops judging her sister's moodiness as a problem and starts accepting it as a sign of her sister's current state of unhappiness, she will see that contesting her sister's behavior only leads to more fighting. The older girl's happiness will be restored when she is able to change or accept herself or do some of both. Parents should teach their children the difference between the blessing of acceptance and the curse of dissatisfaction. *The more self-accepting one is, the more one lives free of problems with oneself. The more self-critical one is, the more ridden with problems (internal conflicts) one becomes.*

Children who are exacting by nature are more prone to bias and intolerance. Parents need to understand that a child's capacity for tolerance falls on a continuum. On one end are those who are very *accepting;* on the other end are those who are very *demanding.* Children who are content, flexible, and grateful for what they have tend to be less critical of themselves and more tolerant of other people. Children who are controlling, critical, and ambitious, however, tend to be harder on themselves and impatient with others. They experience a high degree of conflict because the way other people are is *not* okay with them.

High-demand-only children often so strongly incorporate parental values that they can develop a sense of rectitude that makes it hard for them to tolerate it when others deviate from their core values.[12] Because they are changing more than they want to but at the same time cannot change as much as they would like, adolescents can be plagued by a lot of personal dissatisfaction. They create more problems to contend with, and so parents tend to have more conflicts with their highly conflicted teen than they did when he was a contented child.

Parents need to help their children and adolescents understand that designating any part of one's life as a "problem" sets up a conflict by creating intolerance for how things are when compared with how one wants them to be. For example, an ambitious perfectionist comes home from school unhappy because he failed to get the top test score. After empathizing with the child's hurt feelings, parents might want to help him to understand that while excellence is a good goal, perfection is not the standard by which he should judge the worth of his efforts. "Trying your best is good for you, but believing you should be the best all the time is not, because it's not realistic."

Of course, there are times when the conduct of one family member is implicated in the problem of another, creating conflict between them. For example, children's self-declared problems with parents can be confusing for those adults to deal with, particularly when one child objects to a parent's behavior but another child does not. This can occur when the good-natured teasing from a father that the five-year-old sees as playful, the sixteen-year-old takes as humiliating. Each child chooses to judge it differently. When the teenager bristles at his teasing, the father should say, "I didn't realize my kidding was offensive, and I won't do it anymore." This takes one cause of parent/adolescent conflict off the family table.

Intolerance can have a constructive role with regard to creating problems. In some areas of life, parents want their child to create a problem, to be biased against certain kinds of behaviors, to identify a conflict, and to be able to say: "This is not how I want things to be!" Consider this question: Do you want your teenager in a first love relationship tolerating abusive behavior? The answer is a resounding no! You don't want your child engaging in any kinds of destructive behavior. So you teach a certain amount of healthy intolerance. What an accepting child may permit, a demanding child will not stand for.

Finally, there are situations in which parents reach the end of their patience with a willful child who in their words "runs the family." They don't want to tolerate this behavior any more, but they don't know what to do about the problem. In counseling, I suggest that, at least for the child, "there is no problem, at least not where it needs to be. You have a problem with his lack of cooperation and contribution, but except for your irritation (which is a small price for him to pay) he has no problem with the status quo. So suppose you *give him a problem*. Suppose you change the way things are so they are not as he wants them to be. For example, you could make certain freedoms he enjoys contingent upon the completion of his chores. Create enough conflict between how things are and how he wants them to be and he might be motivated to change his behavior in order to get what he wants."

THREE IDEAS ABOUT *INTOLERANCE AND CONFLICT* TO CARRY FORWARD

- The expression of parental bias (criticism) and parental intolerance (impatience) in response to a child's efforts to acquire a new skill, understanding, or responsibility can create conflicts that can discourage that child's effort to learn at the time, and reduce willingness to learn later on.
- Conflict over developmental differences that increases during adolescence needs to be conducted *below the rejection line* as an opposition of wants and needs to avoid any expressions of criticism or intolerance for

the changing character, values, or habits that increasingly set parents and teenager apart.

- When parents are willing to *bridge differences* between themselves and their adolescent with curiosity and interest, they can turn a disagreement into an opportunity for learning what their teenager, as informant rather than opponent, has to teach them as he or she grows.

5

RESEMBLANCE AND CONFLICT

The dynamics of resemblance, being like or not like someone, are complicated because they can be both the source and the consequence of conflict. Resemblance can *cause* conflict when sibling rivalry prompts children to fight for superiority or a shared objective. Resemblance can *result* from conflict when one party starts imitating the other's tactics and strategies in order to prevail, for example, when a parent uses sarcasm when a teenager is mocking her. *Resemblance can create conflict* and *conflict can create resemblance*.

HOW CONFLICT CREATES RESEMBLANCE

Conflict can create resemblance because it encourages two kinds of imitation.

- There is *imitation of the opponent* for good or ill. Acting in a similar way to the other person in a conflict can be a good thing when it matches the other person's willingness to listen but not good when it means trading criticism or accusations back and forth.
- There is *imitation of past behavior* for good or ill. Acting in a similar manner in a conflict to the way one did before is good when one is calmly sticking to specifics but not good if it means once again backing down in the face of anger.

IMITATION OF THE OPPONENT

Conflict can *encourage* imitative behavior in the participants. One child escalates a verbal disagreement into a physical one by hitting, encouraging the other child to become physical too, until the two are exchanging blow for blow. The longer people fight, the more alike their fighting becomes. "Why did you hit your sister?" asks the parent who wants no hitting in the family. The reply, "Because she hit me first!"

When a person who has been treated badly retaliates in the same tone or manner, it is an example of resemblance. The rule "treat others as you want them to treat you" is often overwhelmed by a "similarity imperative," which says "treat others *as they treat* you." Thus insult begets insult, put-down begets put-down, and blow begets blow. Of course, sometimes the child who picks a fight *wants* the other child to respond in kind to get the conflict started. For children and adults, the temptation to play the game of conflict according to the other person's rules and moves can feel irresistible.

Parents should not underestimate the formative influence of sibling conflict or of conflict between themselves and children. *Resemblance in conflict has evolutionary power to shape behavior.*

One young adult remarked, "I really learned to argue to win by debating my older brother, and I suppose he did with me, at least that's what our wives would say because we've both turned out the same— we're two guys ready to argue with anyone about anything!" In family counseling, it's common to see such mutual imitation causing parent and child to become more alike in the way they handle conflict over time, as each copies some of the other person's characteristic responses. However, with guidance, this process can be constructive. For example, a reticent parent may begin to feel more comfortable about declaring feelings when an explosive child, copying as well, picks up more of the adult's rational restraint.

For parents who grew up passively submissive to an overbearing father or mother, engaging with a willful, confrontational teenager can train them to become more assertive. As one such parent put it, "My son only respects my stands when I firmly defend them. I guess I have to thank him for toughening me up. In our disagreements I've learned to act more like him!"

Parents who encourage a child to imitate them can be intentionally instructive. When parents consistently model respectful listening, calm discourse, staying on the topic, and talking in specifics, the child learns to follow their example. Parents must guard against, however, allowing resemblance to go the other way, imitating the child by voice raising, interrupting, threatening, changing the subject, accusing, or name-calling, particularly when arguing with a strong-willed younger child or an emotionally intense adolescent.

When the adult imitates the child in conflict, immature behavior will often be the order of the day. The child is likely to prevail because he or she is better at it. A nine-year-old matter-of-factly explained how she won most conflicts with her parents, or at least managed to keep things at a standoff. "If I yell at them, I can get them to yell at me, and since I can yell louder and longer than they can, they finally give up and let whatever go." *Be careful not to play by the child's rules.* With a child who yells to get control and get her way, keep talking calmly and softly in the face of the storm until she loses steam and begins to imitate you, becoming quieter and less emotional, more receptive and reasonable. This can take time, but it's worth the effort. When it comes to conducting conflict, you must be the leader. Your child needs to follow your example. The lesson for parents is, *consistently model the behavior you want to receive so that the power of resemblance causes the child to imitate you.*

On the other hand, if you don't like the communication style that you are modeling for your child and see her picking up some of your bad habits, remember the quote attributed to Mahatma Gandhi: "You must be the change you wish to see in the world." So, to help your child change his behavior, change your own.

One father described doing just that in a workshop: "I grew up with parents who were always popping off. They could make the biggest fuss over the smallest problem or disagreement. I suppose I learned my emotional explosiveness from them. So when my kids were young and they did something I didn't like or want, they could predict that Dad would get loud and act upset. And I never really thought much about it until my oldest child, at around twelve years old, started popping off with *me* the way I had always done with her. One day I was driving her over to a friend's house. I just casually mentioned, 'When you get home I want you to fold the laundry and put away the dishes like I asked you to do after breakfast.' She'd reached the age where she put off doing chores as long as possible. Imagine my surprise when she shot back, 'I will not!' I did a mental double take. *What* did she just say? Well, I jammed on the breaks. This was defiance and I wasn't going to stand for it. 'Don't you ever talk that way to me again!' I barked. Then there was this long, quiet pause before she calmly said, 'Dad, get used to it!' And I was about to really lose it again when it occurred to me that she was right, at least about one thing. She now felt old enough to challenge me, and she was doing it the same way I had always challenged her. That's when I realized that we could go toe to toe with each other for the rest of her growing up if that was what I wanted, or we could do something different, but I would have to lead the way. Now it was my turn to be quiet, and then I said, 'Later, we've got some talking to do. Right now I need some time to cool down and think.' And that's what I did. I thought about how I didn't want us exploding at each other all the time like I had done with my parents, and when she got back, I told her so. I promised from then on to listen to whatever she had to say when we got crossways, and said I hoped she could do the same with me because we were going to have lot of differences to settle in the years ahead. She didn't say anything, just listened, looked at me kind of funny, and then got about her chores. But I kept my word, and from then on, for the most part, we talked out our disagreements without either of us heating up and popping off." Breaking free of unhealthy resemblance can be difficult, but it can be done. Did the father in this example wait too long to make this positive change in himself? In the words of Martin Luther King, Jr.: "The time is always right, to do what is right." It is never too late to make a change for the good.

　　By example, you give instruction in how to conduct conflict with other members of the family and by interaction with the child, just as you received instruction from the conflicts with your parents and between them. What I call the power of resemblance, another psychologist refers to as *absorption*: "It is definitely difficult to live in a battle zone without being affected by the hostilities. We absorb the patterns of our parents in the air we breathe. Without our knowledge and consent, the constant exposure to negative ways of reacting instills them in us. They become the default mode of our own behavior, so you find yourself treating your boy friend [spouse or child] the way your mother treats your father, when you don't even meant to."[1] As children, much of what we learn about how to act in conflict is acquired without our knowing it.

In counseling, it is sometimes the adolescent who complains about a parent fighting back in kind (resemblance) because she wants to show mom or dad how hurtful this way of handling disagreement has become. Describing her relationship with her father, a high school senior declares, "One thing for sure, when I make my own home with someone, there's going to be no saying the mean things my Dad and I say to each other!" But I have to disagree. "By giving back to your Dad what he gives you, trading insult for insult and hurt for hurt, you've learned to do conflict the way he does, and that's how you are likely to behave with a partner, unless..." I pause. "Unless what?" she asks. "Unless you resist the pull of imitation. If you train yourself to act differently with your father now, you will be able to do it differently with someone else later on." My job in these situations is to help the young person appreciate the shaping power of resemblance, to see the implications of her present behaviors for her relationships in the future. She can't change her father's behavior, but she doesn't have to let resemblance shape her own.

Consider the agony of an adult daughter who had this to say. "I spent most of my teenage years fighting my mom over behaviors I couldn't stand in her, like her need to control the tiniest things. She refused to let anything go, getting furious when things weren't kept or done exactly right by her standards. I fought to change her every way I could. And what did I get for all my efforts? She hasn't changed a bit, maybe is even worse today. And as for me, I've ended up acting just like my mother. If the smallest things don't go my way, I get really upset." The antidote for "conflict-creating resemblance" is "acceptance-allowing individuality." In this case, if the daughter had been able to accept her mother as she was instead of fighting her at every turn, the younger woman could have declared independence and invested her energy in defining herself a different way.

IMITATION OF PAST BEHAVIOR

Human beings are creatures of habit. More precisely, we are captives of habit, inclined to repeat familiar behaviors without thinking. *Habitual behavior is just resemblance that is created when we do again what we have practiced many times before.* Once rituals and routines (constructive habits) and compulsions and addictions (destructive habits) become established, they can be resistant to change. Habit is efficient because it is automatic. The habits parents learned as children become automatic reflexes as they begin to parent their own children.

Consider the way two parents describe their parents' communication in conflict.

- "My Mom said really hurtful things when we got into fights. She always apologized after, but the damage had been done. I think that's partly why I lose my temper when the kids won't do what I want right away. I act like her."
- "My Dad refused to argue, using threat of punishment to shut any conflict down, or just walking away. That's why it's really hard for me to listen to my kids when we disagree. I find myself acting like him."

Fortunately, the communication style is not fixed once it is learned; we can make a choice to change it. In the case of the adults above, each learned a new way of handling conflict. The first adult was able to moderate her emotional intensity and watch her words. The second adult was able to welcome conflict as an opportunity to understand an opposing point of view. It takes self-awareness and a willingness to make the effort to change, but it's more than possible. You have to work at it, but the rewards are great.

FALLING INTO HABIT'S TRAP

Because intense emotional arousal in conflict can be so commanding, it is tempting to fall into familiar patterns of behavior without thinking.

When you are tired or your child is provocative, it can be hard to pause long enough to be intentional. After any significant conflict with your child, it is worthwhile to ask yourself: "Did I react in a constructive way? Do I wish I had acted differently? If so, how?"

One father described doing just that. Feeling frustrated with his heedless four-year-old daughter, he impulsively "grabbed her arm with angry hands." He didn't hit her or shake her, but his hard grip conveyed a physical threat. "I remember," he soberly recalled, "how my dad used to grab me to get my attention at that age, and how I hated it! I don't want to do this to a child of my own, but in the heat of the moment it's hard to stop." I explained that the only way for him to stop being *reactive* in a way he doesn't like is to become *proactive* in the way he wants. This entails making a *plan* for acting differently the next time his child acts thoughtlessly or recklessly. In this case, his initial plan was to get in front of the child, crouch down so she would be on eye level, smile, hold out his hands for the girl to take, and say, "I love you very much, and this is what I need to have you do."

Would this work? He considered it worth the effort. If it didn't work, he was free to try something else. In conflicts between parent and child, the party with the most choices wields the most influence because that person keeps changing the nature of the interaction. In this case the father continually gives his daughter different adult behaviors to respond to. As the girl adjusts to changes in her father, she starts relating more on her father's terms. To break the hold of habitual behavior in conflict, take yourself off "automatic pilot" and intentionally act differently.

Sometimes parents need a "prescription" to break the hold of resemblance in conflict, to stop repeating behavior that encourages the child to fight harder. The parents' force of habit keeps playing into the child's hands. Consider the mother who described how her fourteen-year-old son was exploiting his new physical growth and manly stature to intimidate her into giving him his way. "Now that he's bigger," she complained, "he often bullies me into backing down."

The first step in helping her deal with this problem was to have her specify the behaviors in her son that she found threatening, since there's no such thing as a self-made bully. She described his moving so close that his face was almost touching hers, staring hard into her eyes, giving his mouth an angry snarl, raising his voice, giving her orders, hunching his shoulders, waving his arms, and starting to walk into her when she began to talk. This was threatening behavior indeed. The second step was getting her to specify how she thought her son predicted she would respond. She described how he would expect her to widen her eyes in fright, slump her shoulders, seem to "shrink" and back away from him, to raise her hands protectively and to plead with him to stop in a faint voice. Now we were ready for step three. Could she act in a way that would violate his prediction, giving him a response to bullying he did not anticipate and might not want? We came up with this plan. The next time he got "in her face," she would stand up straight, put a big smile on her face, move closer to him, look him in the eyes with great affection, place her hands on his shoulders, pull him to her, kiss him on the cheek and say, "I just love you when you act like this!" The plan worked. When he tried to intimidate her, it began to provoke a loving engagement with his mother instead of fearful backing down. Over time this unpredicted and unwanted response discouraged repetition of his bullying.

When you repeatedly find yourself on the receiving end of unwanted behavior from your child, it is always worth asking yourself what reaction she anticipates. Then formulate a dissimilar response that violates that prediction. One doctor offered a similar ploy he used with parents to discourage adolescent debate. "A simple strategy to defuse tension is to take up the other side of an argument. Just start arguing for the same side your 'opponent' is arguing and see how long it takes him or her to figure it out."[2]

Violating a prediction can also open conflict up for discussion. A teenager sneaked out of bed to rendezvous with friends for a night of adventure. He planned to be back home before his parents woke up, but at 5:00 A.M. the downstairs lights were on. He knew he was caught, so he decided to tough it out with parents who had been furious with him before when he violated rules. He would put the blame for his behavior on their excessive restrictions and over-protectiveness before they could blame him. Ready for a fight, he charged into the house and slammed the door to announce his arrival. But his plan fell apart because they didn't act the way he expected them to. Instead of acting angry, his mother hugged him: "I'm glad you're home safe!" Instead of yelling, his father acted worried, asking: "Is everything okay? Are you all right?" Where their blame would have led to his defensiveness, their concern encouraged him to take responsibility. And what would have been a typical argument turned into a meaningful discussion.

Breaking patterns of resemblance can be a powerful first step in resolving conflict. But this is just the story: Resemblance can also create conflict.

HOW RESEMBLANCE CREATES CONFLICT

Resemblance can create conflict because it encourages three kinds of stubborn opposition: face-offs, conversion conflicts, and rivalries. *Face-offs* occur when the parent and child battle each other based on a shared characteristic. *Conversion conflicts* occur when parents insist on forcing a child to follow the same agenda that they followed growing up. *Sibling rivalries* are sustained when siblings vie for the same reward—be it dominance, parental approval, or possession of a desirable resource.

FACE-OFFS

There are endless varieties of face-offs in which resemblance between the parties obstructs the resolution of conflict. Two proud childhood friends each believe that whenever they argue over something, the other one must admit complicity first. Each one waits the other out: "I won't speak to her until she calls me first!" Then there are the verbose parent and the verbose child who won't shut up, or the silent parent and the silent child who won't speak up, each pair "facing off," that is, exhibiting similar characteristics that make disagreements difficult, if not impossible, to discuss. There is not enough willingness to listen in the first parent-child case and not enough willingness to talk in the second.

A father explained the constant conflict between his wife and adolescent daughter this way. "They're both so stubborn and fixed in their beliefs. Each one has to have her way. Being strong-willed in childhood worked out since our daughter liked to please her mother. Now that she's a teenager, that's the last thing she wants. Now she likes to challenge her mom, and my wife refuses to back down because she's the authority. She is as determined that our daughter will obey her as our daughter is to resist her mom's demands. It's not what they disagree over that's the problem. It's how they do it. When they square off they are so alike. Not giving in is more important to both of them than working anything out." That's what happens in face-offs. Similar characteristics collide to make the conflict intractable.

Adults often experience face-offs as *senseless conflicts* because they don't seem to be about the issue, yield no resolution, and provide no emotional relief. For some parents, face-offs are a painful look in the mirror. In the words of one father who fought to force remorse from his unapologetic daughter and could not bring himself to apologize, "It's like being at war with myself. I'm trying to correct in her what I can't overcome in me."

What often inflames an adolescent in face-offs with a parent is an implied double standard. The parent is "allowed to" display the very same trait that the child is being told to change.

- "Don't interrupt!"
- "Don't criticize!"
- "Don't raise your voice!"

"Well you do!" charges the teenager, "so why shouldn't I?"

From what I have seen in counseling, the "do as I say, not as I do" response fails to resolve most face-offs. A more productive way out of resemblance-based conflicts is for the parent to take the lead. During a quiescent period in their relationship, the parent can discuss the shared trait with the similar son or daughter. There are some simple steps to follow.

- Recognize and describe the trait you and your child seem to share. "We can both be very stubborn when we are opposed."
- Value the positive aspects of this trait. "Being stubborn, you and I are both very persistent in pursuing what we want. We don't give up easily."

- Identify any costs you have found this trait to have in your own life. "There have been times when I have pushed so hard to get what I wanted that I hurt someone I cared about, and I do not want that to happen to us."
- Signify a willingness to conduct the conflict differently. "When we argue I still want to have my say, but I no longer need to have the last word. You can have it if you'd like."
- Propose using the shared trait in a more constructive way. "Maybe we could harness our stubbornness, the two of us refusing to give up until we find a way to work things out."

By taking the lead, the parent also models an alternative response, giving a child who is accustomed to resembling the parent a different example to imitate. One of the most common issues in parent and young child conflict is the volume at which the exchange takes place, which tends to get louder as the conflict wears on. However, when the parent starts speaking softly, it is not long before the young child learns to do the same.

CONVERSION CONFLICTS

If face-offs can feel senseless, conversion conflicts can arise when the parent resents the child for not following his path. In this case, the parent *wants* resemblance, and this agenda collides with the adolescent's agenda—to avoid resemblance to his parents. The issue is who knows best.

Raising children who are different from themselves, in different circumstances, and during a different time in history, parents still use what they know or would like to have known to make decisions about what is best for their children. To some degree, this guidance drawn from their personal past seems serviceable when children develop in ways parents find familiar and productive. This can lull parents into committing what one psychologist aptly describes as "the mistake of thinking everyone is like you."[3] Consider what happens when a child diverges from the resemblance a parent holds dear, like the successful father who wanted his sons to follow in his footsteps. The father attributed his adult success to being a high-performing student, recognized social leader, and varsity athlete in high school. His older son is like him. But the man worries about his younger son, who does only enough to get by in school, is solitary except for a couple of close friends, and creative but not interested in sports. How is he going to get into a good college with that attitude?

The stage was set for a conversion conflict when the dad tried to encourage resemblance by offering incentives and penalizing lack of resemblance. But neither tactic worked as the son steadfastly resisted the father at every turn. In counseling, the father would angrily explain how he wanted the boy to get the most out of his education, as he had. But the son angrily insisted that he didn't care about college and it was his life, not his dad's. Although neither side could ever quite accept the other's position, the resentment fell away over time as each came to see the other as well meaning, just misguided. The son saw that his father wasn't motivated by vanity to create in the son a reflection of himself. He recognized that his father was genuinely interested in helping and that his father believed it was his responsibility to set him on a productive life path. And the father saw that his son wasn't motivated by a need to rebel. He recognized that the boy was determined to be treated like a young man who is mature enough to live by his own decisions. Years later the father told me, "I finally gave up trying to change my younger son into another me. And you know what? He's made his own way and is doing all right for himself. I've learned that there are more ways to move up in the world than I ever imagined. I thought I knew best; but all I really knew was what had worked for me. He had to discover what worked for him. Now that he has, we don't have that to fight about any more." *Conversion conflicts are usually resolved by the parent finally letting go.* The parent has to accept that *informing* the child's choice is the parent's responsibility, but *controlling* the child's choice takes that responsibility too far. It is ultimately up to the child to makes his own decisions.

SIBLING RIVALRY

Parents also have some letting go to do when it comes to sibling rivalries, which are often rooted in competition over resemblance as siblings vie for parental attention and approval, with the same goal of dominance over each other. One writer has observed, "Fighting with a sibling is a normal part of childhood, and surveys suggest that young children have about five conflicts in a day...."[4] The contest begins as soon as the first child is dethroned to make room for a second child. It continues as the number of children in the family increases or the number of parents diminishes through abandonment, death, or divorce. Parents can feel impatient with the discord of these ongoing rivalries, torn by divided loyalties, and challenged when called upon to settle disputes without appearing to favor one side over the other. Probably no aspect of having multiple children wearies parents more than the continuing strife between siblings.

For parents, sibling conflict can be costly in four ways.

1. It can be stressful to be around the unrelenting tension that continual sibling conflict creates.
2. It can deplete parents' energy to monitor, mediate, and otherwise manage sibling conflict.
3. Fatigue from coping with bickering children can affect parental attitude in a more negative and critical way.
4. Sibling conflict can be contagious when hostility between children creates irritability between parents, and between parents and other children.

Conflicts that parents wish would stop, however, may be part of what children rely on to nourish their own growth. *Rivalry is not the same as enmity.* When people are enemies, they usually want to subjugate or somehow destroy the other person, or at least put an end to the relationship. When people are rivals, they want to keep the relationship going because challenging each other has value and is even a form of companionship. Enemies are out to get each other, but rivals trying to best each other spur each other on. To determine whether your children are rivals or enemies, check out their behavior when they are not fighting. If they can enjoy each other's company when not in conflict, they are rivals.

Consider the mother of constantly fighting, fraternal twin daughters who worried out loud that they would "grow up hating each other."

Both girls were surprised at their mother's take on their strife. One of them explained: "Oh Mom, fighting together doesn't mean we don't get along. It's *how* we get along. We'd rather fight with each other than anybody else!" Conflict wasn't driving them apart. It was just one way they had of being together.

As two well-versed writers on the topic note: "Everything we read made a case for the uses of some conflict between brothers and sisters. From their struggles to establish dominance over each other, siblings become tougher and more resilient. From their endless roughhousing with each other, they develop speed and agility. From their verbal sparring they learn the difference between being clever and being hurtful. From the normal irritations of living together, they learn to assert themselves, defend themselves, and compromise. And sometimes, from their envy of each other's special abilities, they become inspired to work harder, persist and achieve. That's the best of sibling rivalry. The worst of it, as parents were quick to tell us, could seriously demoralize one or both of the children and even cause permanent damage."[5]

The task of parents is to appreciate the benefits, moderate the risks, and keep the incidence of sibling conflict within parental tolerance limits, separating the combatants when the adults, not the children, need the relief of a timeout. Sibling conflict that can entertain and energize children can be discouraging and exhausting for parents. But as one of the twins explained, sibling conflict is *not* a sign of children not getting along; it is how they test themselves, defend differences, protest what they don't like, and vent unhappiness.

A creative intervention one mother shared at a workshop is worth mentioning here. Two early elementary-age siblings told their mother that the reason they didn't stop fighting was because "we couldn't, even if we wanted to." "Are you telling me that you can't help fighting?" she asked. "Yes," they agreed, and started poking each other again. "I see what you mean," she said, "and it looks like you're right. So I want you to continue your fight outside, and I will shut the door. Only the one who wins will be allowed back inside." Somewhat startled, the two children filed out the door. In about three minutes there came a knock. "Yes?" answered the mother. "We want to come back in," said a voice. "Sure," she agreed, "one of you, the one who won. Who won?" There was an awkward silence. "No one won," said the other voice, "we didn't fight." "Why not?" asked the mother, acting surprised. Now the second voice chimed in. "Because coming back inside was too important to fight about." The mother waited almost a full minute before responding. "So you both *can* help fighting after all?" In unison came the reluctant reply, "I guess so." And she opened the door and let both children back inside. *Inevitable as it is, sibling conflict is still a matter of mutual choice, and parents need to hold children accountable for that decision.*

The prime motivations for sibling rivalry seem to be

- competition over sharing,
- contesting for dominance,
- companionship through conflict, and
- controlling the age difference between them.

The competition over sharing arises when use of a valued resource like the family computer must be divided or an unwanted responsibility like a chore must be undertaken jointly. The contest for dominance arises when children are playing games or deciding who should be socially in charge. Companionship arises when fighting provides children with a better alternative than each having nothing to do. Controlling the age difference arises when the older sibling resents the younger one for getting certain freedoms earlier than he did or the younger sibling resents the older one for getting privileges he is denied. The younger child may push for equality by copying the older child, who resents this imitation and teases the younger to keep his rival in an inferior place.

In general, the greater the age difference between siblings, the less active rivalry is likely to occur. The most intense rivalries are between same-sex siblings who are close in age and have much in common to contest. (However, this is not true for most identical twins, who often seem to enjoy closeness from sharing similarity.) Otherwise, the more diversity of interests and separation of activities between siblings that parents can encourage, the less intense the rivalry is likely to be.

Just as seniority is the enemy of change in organizations, where long-term employees protect their influence and status against the inroads of new hires, so the first child will defend her turf, dominating the younger to retain her primacy and remain in charge. The first child rarely wants to share, much less surrender, her throne to the next child in line, who sooner or later will contest this supremacy. I strongly agree with the opinion of one knowledgeable writer that "one of the biggest mistakes parents make is always expecting children to resolve their own conflicts."[6]

While it is important for parents to accept sibling conflicts as a fact of life, they do have several response responsibilities when their children are fighting. Parents should

- *moderate* the frequency of sibling conflict by creating adequate separation between them, as much for their own sake as for the kids, who need the respite of some time and space apart;
- *mediate* disputes that are beyond the children's capability to resolve or that are escalating to a point of emotional harm; and
- *monitor* physical safety, making sure neither child gives or receives injury.

Parents who do not adequately monitor sibling conflict can appear to condone the mistreatment of one child by the other. The child who is typically the aggressor is more likely to be aggressive in other conflicts as an adult, while the child who is generally the victim is more likely to accept the passive role later on. When parents tolerate one sibling continually harming another in conflict they are at risk of having an adult child who finds it very hard to forgive them for refusing to stop what they never should have allowed. A policy that directs children to work all disagreements out by themselves and forbids them from bothering their parents, that is, forbids tattling, is not sound. Siblings often need adult governance when their disputes have gotten, or are likely to get, out of hand.

A responsible role for parents is to teach rival children that fighting can be a very costly way to settle a disagreement because one of them will lose and feel unhappy about it, and, worse, one or both may get emotionally or physically hurt. One mother of two contentious sons, ages seven and eight, wanted them to understand how they had many other choices for resolving their conflicts besides fighting. To make this point, she posted a list of what she called "Ten Peaceful Ways to Solve Your Disagreements" to which she would refer them when inevitable differences between the two siblings arose. The list looked like this.

- "Some of my way and some of your way" = compromise.
- "This time I'll go along with your way" = concession.
- "We'll do it your way this time and my way next time" = exchange.
- "We'll play two out of the three and the winner gets to decide" = competition.
- "We'll leave the disagreement alone and do something else" = acceptance.
- "We'll figure out another way we both like" = collaboration.
- "We'll let someone else decide which way" = help.
- "We'll flip a coin to decide which way" = chance.
- "We'll just listen to each other explain their way" = understanding.
- "One of us will pay the other something to get their way" = buyout.

The mother wanted the two siblings to know that they had many other choices for working out their differences than automatic fighting. Fighting is predicated on three assumptions: might is right, the strongest wins, and winner takes all. What she was encouraging were other approaches that could help her sons get along better.

To moderate the incidence and intensity of sibling rivalry, and to maximize the good effects, there are some basic principles that parents might want to keep in mind.

- to establish sufficient separation in time and space between children so they can have adequate independence of each other,
- to nurture authentic differences between children so each has a sense of individuality that eases competition over similarity,
- to create opportunities for valued interactions between them so companionship can develop into friendship,
- to arrange for siblings to have separate, uncontested time with each parent for individual attention,

- to not make comparisons between children that evaluate one child positively or negatively,
- to not show preference for the company of one child or the performance of one child over another, and
- to not play favorites by investing more attention, time, effort, or resources in one child than in another.

When parents make a comparison, "Why can't you act like your sister?" or express a preference, "I like your brother's idea better than yours," or show favoritism, "We give her more because she deserves it," they inflame the rivalry. The most acute sibling rivalries I have seen are those deliberately abetted by a parent who provokes competition by playing "divide for dominance." This approach pits the kids against each other with constantly shifting statements of comparison, preference, and favoritism. This inconsistency causes them to ruthlessly compete for primary attachment to the manipulative adult, who remains in family control at significant long-term cost. Siblings who have been raised this way often declare independence from parents in adulthood, no longer concerned about earning their favor, and they often confront their own estrangement. Then they cease their sibling conflict, attempt reconciliation, and hold the manipulative parent accountable for fostering the divisive rivalry.

Some of the most intractable sibling rivalries arise when parents favor a child who is similar to them, and who acts how they want, over a *troublesome* one who acts differently. Now one sibling is cast in the role of the "good" child and the other as the "bad." Consider how this unhappy circumstance can develop.

THE "GOOD" CHILD VERSUS
THE "BAD" CHILD

All children eventually feel social pressure to conform, but that pressure often begins at home. As the standard bearers of family values and the resident powers-that-be, parents set the terms on which the little boy or girl is expected to live. To the child, similarity to these adults feels rewarding on two powerful counts. First, sense of alikeness increases sense of affiliation with parents, and second, it usually meets with their approval.

Commonality with and obedience to parents are powerful expressions of resemblance. The child deemed easiest to live with is the one who appears most temperamentally similar to them and acts the way they want. For example, consider the child who is the obliging "pleaser" and the child who is the resistant "pusher." Parents are likely to find the child who is conciliatory and eager to please easier to parent than the child who is willful and is determined to contest their requests, rules, and restraints. Parental favoritism tends to favor both obedience and resemblance.

Favoritism can be very seductive for parents. They enjoy the feeling of commonality, familiarity, and compatibility with the similar child. They may say, "With our oldest we have always matched, viewed and valued things the same way, and felt closely connected." They like seeing themselves reflected in this child, who likes resembling them. Now look more closely at what happens when there is significant diversity between parents and another child. The first-born child is strongly built like both parents, is also outspoken and socially inclined, has the same high energy level, and loves to compete. In addition, child number one is eager to learn game-playing skills from parents, enjoys their outdoor interests, is generally compliant and cooperative, and assimilates their devotion to watching and participating in all kinds of popular sports. Parents and child take great pleasure in sharing so much with each other.

Then along comes child number two who is different from child number one, and thus different from the parents. More reflective and shy, lethargic and easily tired, favoring reading and fantasy games over outdoor sports, more private and less communicative, the second child is also stubborn. He can be very resistant when asked to interrupt absorbing solitary play.

It isn't that the parents love child number two less than child number one, but in counseling they agree that number two "is our more difficult child." This judgment becomes stronger when number two has followed number one into adolescence. In counseling, parents say, "Our first child talks to us, gets good grades, is fun to be with. But our second stays in his room and acts irritated when we want him to come out and join the family or get homework or housework done. All he wants is to be left alone to pursue things that don't interest us. We end up trying to get him to go along with us, which he refuses to do. So much of our communication is argumentative."

The frustration parents feel over the child's dissimilarity to them often escalates during adolescence. The teenager stubbornly defends his refusal to fit into the family: "I'm not like both of you and my sister, and I'm not going to be!" Now a harmful change in perception is likely to occur. When parents judge one child "easy" based on resemblance and another "difficult" based on divergence from the family norm, they are in danger of equating *similar* with *good* and *different* with *bad*. They increasingly give the "good" child "positive reviews" and rewards, and the "bad" child more "negative reviews" and correction. Feeling unfairly treated, the "bad" child may grow angry at the perceived injustice, increasing his negative reputation. At the same time, by becoming a lightning rod for conflict in the family, he can monopolize parental attention.

The contrasting roles played by each child often give rise to jealousy-based conflict between them. The bad child envies the parental approval and the benefits received for "good citizenship." The good child envies the greater amount of parental attention devoted to the bad child and the special exceptions to wrongdoing, and all the second chances. The parents do not mean to be unfair. They are trying their best to straighten the bad child out. However, by now their attempt takes the form of criticism, correction, and negative consequences, which cause that child, in self-defense, to become resistant and combative. *When some children are favored based on resemblance to parents and others are disfavored for not being similar enough, parent/child conflict and sibling conflict can become more frequent and intense.*

The good child/bad child distinction can be extremely destructive. Ironically, the good child often pays the greater cost. How? Consider what can happen at the end of adolescence. At this juncture, the "bad" child can claim the individuality for which he or she has always fought. He can honestly say, "You have known me at my worst," make amends to his parents, and proceed on a positive footing with them. At last out of the business of active parenting, they can give up the battle and accept their more difficult child for who he is. They are able to appreciate the good in the child since they no longer feel obliged to change the bad. He may even be treated like a prodigal son returned.

In contrast, the good child may have sacrificed individuality and authenticity in trying to maintain the parents' favor all these years. To avoid the criticism the bad child received, the good child usually suppresses her own different or difficult side. Approaching but never crossing the threshold of independence, the good child feels trapped. She commits herself to living up to her parents' idealized image of her because she fears losing their love and approval. In counseling, such an adult will declare, "I never could bear displeasing or disappointing them, and I still can't!" *When a good child, in deliberate contrast to the bad child, denies herself authenticity and independence for the sake of gaining parental approval, there is a high price to pay. Having loyally lived up to their expectations, she may experience a painful lack of individuality as an adult.*

The adult good child's envy of her sibling can come out in counseling, along with resentment: "I wish I'd had the courage to be a problem child, to battle my parents and dare to do what they forbade!" The good child sees the bond between the adult bad child and his parents that comes from having made it though the hard times. The parents did not have to make this special effort with the good child, who feels taken for granted. When the adult good child lets some of her bad side out and incurs their disappointment, it may seem to her that her prodigal sibling is now favored and she is the fallen angel.

For the bad child, growing up with parental disapproval can cause him to become self-rejecting. "How am I supposed to feel good about myself when my parents didn't like me?" he asks. The good child, however, has her own painful question to ask. "How can I feel good about being who I truly am if it lets my parents down?" Neither child wins this competition.

The good child/bad child dynamic is neither a valid nor a healthy distinction. To loosen its grip and reduce its attendant conflicts, parents can send two important messages.

- To the "good"-acting child, parents can communicate that sometimes "letting her more difficult side out" is okay and that misbehavior will not jeopardize her positive standing in their eyes or lessen their love.
- To the "bad"-acting child, parents can communicate that no matter how troublesome they may find his behavior sometimes, it is only a minor part of a larger person they value highly, and they can identify and appreciate his positive traits.

How can parents tell whether they have fallen into this resemblance trap with their children? If you have one child who has never given you one moment of concern and another who has been nothing but trouble, you may have the good child/bad child dynamic at work in your family. If you have one child who has only been a joy and another who has been a source of constant aggravation, you may have the good child/bad child dynamic at work. If you have one child who has always conscientiously done things just the way you like and another who has challenged every household rule, you may have the good child/bad child dynamic at work.

To keep this destructive distinction from playing out, parents need to accept that their children's resemblance to or diversity from themselves is part of the family mix. To grow into the fullness of self, each child needs room to conform and not conform to his parents, to be both easy *and* difficult, and to be the good child who sometimes behaves badly.

THREE IDEAS ABOUT
RESEMBLANCE AND CONFLICT
TO CARRY FORWARD

- Since conflict creates resemblance by encouraging adversaries to imitate each other's influential tone and tactics, parents should make sure they model in conflict the behavior they want the child to learn to use.

- Resemblance creates conflict by provoking *face-offs* between a parent and child who have similar traits, by causing *conversion conflicts* when parents demand a child follow their agenda or example, and by arousing *rivalries* between siblings who fight for dominance.
- Rivalry between siblings is *not* enmity; it is *how* they get along, establishing diversity from each other, competing against each other, ventilating frustrations with each other, and enjoying each other's company between conflicts.

6

CHANGE AND CONFLICT

Of the eight factors in conflict described in this book, none precipitates more disagreement between parents and child than *change*—that process that keeps upsetting and resetting the terms of everyone's existence. The new cultural styles and technological advances that children embrace at best confound their parents and at worst offend them, causing generational conflict. Family change that parents initiate, like deciding to have another child, geographically move, or divorce, can be opposed by children who want to keep living conditions the same. Child rearing itself creates constant conflict as parents try to stay current with the child's unfolding growth, welcoming development that brings more maturity, but contesting abrasive behaviors like those that tend to accompany adolescence. When parent or child resist change in each other, conflict can result.

THE NATURE OF CHANGE

Change operates in four ways:

- *Something new* is started, like adding a child to the family (a beginning).

- *Something old* is stopped, like leaving elementary school (an ending).
- *Something more* is added, like additional chores (an increase).
- *Something less* is endured, like reduced time with a working parent (a decrease).

The periods of highest stress in people's lives tend to be when all four kinds of changes are operating at once. For example, a parent who has just divorced (an ending) has to find a new job (a beginning) while dealing with more parenting responsibilities (an increase) with less income (a decrease).

Children in this situation can also be under stress. They may have to get used to traveling between two homes (a beginning), mourn the loss of their nuclear family (an ending), accept more household responsibilities in each single-parent home (an increase), and see each parent less (a decrease). Times of family change can wear down people's resilience, making them irritable and likely to argue over even normal slights and frustrations. Feeling less in control, parent and child may fight to regain it. Immediately after divorcing, many single parents in counseling report an increase in conflict with children over the family reorganization. There may be more sibling conflict until everyone gets accustomed to the new family circumstances and arrangements. And when remarriage creates one household out of two, children of each parent usually go through some conflict with each other as they jockey for position in the reconstituted family.

Coping with major family change requires three kinds of hard adjustments:

- *giving up* the old and suffering pain from loss and grief,
- *getting lost* in transition and suffering confusion and uncertainty,
- *going forward* burdened by doubt and anxiety about coping with what's new and unknown.

People's tolerance of change can vary with life experience. An only child who has had a constant, steady home life may be more resistant to change than siblings with a parent in the military, who, having to move every two years, have become resilient.

ACCEPTING CHANGE

Change is challenging but inevitable, and we must do it all our lives. Between parent and child, change becomes divisive when one party wants the new while the other wants the old, when one party pushes for reformation while the other defends the status quo. "Why do we have to do holidays the same old way every year?" objects the adolescent who now finds tradition boring. To which parents, who love repeating these rituals, answer, "Because we always have."

Change creates conflict because its demands are often resisted. Just think of the litany of conflicts over freedom that arise as the healthy child, particularly the healthy adolescent, pushes for *new* room to grow and healthy parents insist that some *old* family rules, regulations, and restraints remain in place, for safety's sake. It is as difficult for parents to adjust to new aspects of their child's growth as it is for the child to tolerate old limits parents still impose. The resulting conflict is always about opposition between the old and the new.

Typically, the child initiates conflict in order to get more freedom, and parents initiate conflict to insist on more responsibility. This is the ongoing contest between parent and child that developmental changes of childhood ordain. A common clash between freedom and responsibility occurs when parental expectations shift as the child grows older. For example, when she was very young, parents may have asked their only child to do very little for herself or for them. They mistakenly expected that she would want to make contributions as she got older. At age nine, however, she has become accustomed to being indulged, while her parents want her to begin picking up after herself, cleaning her room, and helping with household chores. In counseling they want to know: "Is this asking too much?" My reply is, "Only if it's too much for you to defend your new stand, because that is what you may have to do. She will resist changing privileges to which she has come to feel entitled. So expect some combination of complaint, argument, refusal, and delay. Conflict is the price you're going to have to pay for this new contribution from your daughter. She will protect her old freedoms and protest these new responsibilities." The question to consider is how to implement the changes you want. This usually includes presenting the child with the four C's:

- *cause* for the change,
- *clarity* about what they are asking for,
- *consistency* in supervision to make sure those changes occur, and
- *compliments* every time she starts complying with the new regime.

Parents should not challenge complaints or punish noncompliance with their request for change, since both responses are likely to intensify opposition. What usually works better is for the parents to listen to what she has to say, but then repeatedly insist on getting their way, using that insistence to wear down her resistance. The child has a name for this relentless pursuit. "Stop *nagging* me, I hate it when you nag me!" They reply, "We will stop nagging you when you do as we ask." Although tiring to give and irritating to receive, nagging is an effective part of supervision. It shows that parents are determined to keep after the child until she complies with the change they want. It shows they are serious, mean what they say, and will invest unflagging energy in accomplishing their objective. They will not let it go, they will not give up, and they will not back down. Nagging works, as testified by the twelve-year-old who finally stopped refusing the regimen of dental care required for her new braces. Although she wanted her teeth to be straight, daily cleaning this hardware was a change she had been steadfastly resisting. So I asked her, "Why did you finally give in to your parents on this?" Her reply: "Because I got tired of them hassling me and wanted to get them off my back!" Because nagging is so exhausting and unrewarding to do, parents should share the onerous responsibility. Otherwise, the child will treat the nagging parent as the "mean" one and the non-nagging parent as the "nice" one who will let her get away with things. This distinction can become divisive in the marriage: "I do all the supervision and you do none!" Then conflict with the child causes conflict between the parents. *When parents want to change a behavior the child wishes to continue, they must commit to calm, firm, consistent supervision.* Parents must also be prepared to have their child initiate conflict with them when he resists the course of action they have chosen to take and objects to unwanted family change.

FAMILY-CHANGE CONFLICTS

Children have to live on parents' terms because they depend on parents for support. One result of this dependency, in the words of one young child in counseling, is being "yanked around" by parental changes that can alter living conditions for the child. Parents move, take a new job, have another child, develop a major interest outside of home, commit to some schedule or personal growth plan, get divorced, get remarried, make a host of individual and family decisions. In the course of the life changes they make, parents are constantly upsetting and resetting the terms of their child's existence. When the child resists the change, to protect the old way or to protest the new one, parents can get impatient with him for not getting with the new program. When they resist with criticism, correction, or consequences, opposition between them is intensified.

It helps avoid unnecessary conflict over family change if parents understand, respect, and work with the child's resistance instead of resisting in return and inciting conflict. *Resistance is functional* for the child in a number of ways. It expresses opposition and registers objection. It buys time for adjustment. It asserts power to affect influence. And it expresses a variety of hard emotions. All four functions create worthwhile talking points for the parent.

- "Can you tell me all the ways this change is something you don't want?"
- "If we could slow this change down, what amount of time would you need?"
- "How could we modify this change to make it more workable for you?"

- "Would you tell me some of the hard feelings that this change creates?"

When encountering a child's resistance to a family change, the parent's first order of business is discussing the difficult adjustments that will be involved. Respect the child's resistance so he is more open to talking and less inclined to act out. Parents should help children understand that any major life change is a *compromise* that mixes what is *different* with what remains the *same*. In this sense, no matter how devoutly wanted or unwanted, change is usually a broken promise— never quite as good as one hoped or as bad as one feared. *Continuity limits family change* because habit and history carry old beliefs and behaviors forward into new situations. Just as the future is always built upon the past, the new is constructed from the old.

When the second-grade child vows to fight the move to a new city because "everything will be different and I won't go!" parents can reduce this resistance by describing how continuity will moderate the change. They can explain how much of life before the move will still be in place after the move. The formula for change is not *change = different*; the formula is *change = same + different*. Not only that: It will be *more* the same than different. Family members and the way the family functions will remain the same. The extended family will remain the same. The family history will remain the same. Any new school she goes to will be much like the old one. Still the child protests, "I won't have any friends, it will be totally different!" But there is an answer for that. "You will still have your old friendships, and we will help you keep up with them. Most of what will be different is making new friends, and we will help you with that as well." With young children, resistant to unwanted family change,

- emphasize continuity,
- place what is different in a realistic perspective, and
- offer strategies to help your child adjust to her new experiences.

Another strategy is to help the child see beyond the costs of change to possible benefits. "What benefits?" argues the child. "There are no benefits!" To which the parent can truthfully reply, "There are always some." In the new situation there will be some *freedom from* old constraints (she won't need to be so quiet now that they are in a house and not an apartment with neighbors). And there will be *freedom for* new opportunities (she can have a dog now that they have a yard). Get the child involved in thinking about the positive aspects of change using her own words, "What I don't have to do anymore" and "What I get to do that I couldn't do before." Unwanted change can usually be exploited to positive effect.

Family change affects every family member differently, and it helps to be sensitive to this reality. Consider a single parent's remarriage. This change may be supported by a young child who is prepared to bond with her new stepparent. But it may feel decidedly unwelcome to her adolescent older sister whose loyalty to the absent parent makes her unwilling to attach to a parent substitute. The same change has a very different impact on each child. The older child may even fight with the younger child for accepting a stepparent who she believes should have no loving standing in their eyes, and thus for betraying the biological parent. The older child may express her feelings by acting standoffish. The parent and stepparent need to respect this passive form of resistance. It is going to take time for the teenager to get used to the new family constellation.

Finally, when it comes to change that the child wants, parents need to do their best to forestall future conflict by exercising their *predictive responsibility*. Consider the teenager who wants to put the money he has saved toward buying a car. He is excited at the prospect of having his own "wheels." Parents, however, understand that *change is just a process of substitution*, replacing old problems and payoffs with new ones. All their son can see is that an old problem (having to depend upon parents for rides) will go away, and a new payoff (freedom and independence) will be created. Parents need to reduce the likelihood that conflict will arise from the surprise of inaccurate expectations. They look at the hardships that their son's desired change can create—the advantages that will be lost (like free transportation) and the new problems created (like the responsibilities and the expense of operating a car).

Parents have to teach the young person that major life change can not only create conflict between people, as it often does between parent and child, but also create conflict within people. Even when someone wants a change very much, he can feel sincere *ambivalence*. The little boy wants to go away to an overnight summer camp but feels torn because he will miss his parents and friends. Parents need to honor these mixed feelings by explaining that many changes in life involve tradeoffs, having to endure something difficult to get to enjoy something good.

TIMING CONFLICTS

To get what she wants from parents, a child depends on their provision and permission. To get what they want from her, parents depend on her cooperation and compliance. In this sense, each party is at the other's mercy all through childhood and adolescence. The result is constant tension around the issue of change over what one party wants *now* and what the other wants to postpone until later. Immediate gratification is at stake for them both.

When parents ask for a room to be picked up now, the nine-year-old cheerfully agrees: "Sure I will, in just a minute. After I've finished playing my game." And as "now" becomes later and the minute stretches into an hour, the parent's patience stretches thin. He realizes that he rarely gets what he wants from his child right away.

Consider what happens when the child wants permission to do something with a friend who has just called with an invitation. Busy with other concerns, the parent puts off a decision. "Give me some time to think about it, and we can talk about it in a little while." Soon "a little while" takes so long that the window of opportunity starts to close, so the child starts pestering the parent for a decision. On this point parents and child agree: Nothing is happening now. It takes pestering by the child and nagging by the parent to keep later from lasting forever.

The resolution over when a change is going to occur, now or later, is the aggravating, all-purpose compromise, *delay*. Reluctantly, both parties learn to wait for what they want because the timing of request and response is rarely right. How often does one party immediately provide for what the other party wanted? Not very frequently. This frustration from the timing conflicts is part of transacting daily business with each other. It will never go away. The same is true for conflicts that keep arising as a function of the child's developmental change.

DEVELOPMENTAL CONFLICTS

Growth alters children's capacities, desires, and behaviors. To avoid unnecessary conflict, our ongoing task as parents is to anticipate, accept, and adjust to those changes as our children grow. After all, the infant does not remain content to be carried in our arms. She is programmed to crawl and then walk, and this developmental process continues through childhood and adolescence, when she is programmed to claim more separation from our care. At each developmental milestone, such as imitating language and soon learning to use words to satisfy her needs, a child's way of functioning changes. It is important for parents to be aware of these changes so they can respond to a child's new behaviors appropriately. For example, defiance in a two-year-old who has discovered the word "no" is age-appropriate and the result of her newfound sense of independence. Another age of "no" returns seven or eight years later when the early adolescent becomes more rebellious against being treated like a child anymore.

In dealing with such changes in our children, we must distinguish changes that are a function of this natural developmental process and those that are a matter of choice. Parents should not correct their child for growing up, but they should hold him accountable for how he manages his behavior so they can help guide his development. For example, it is normal in early childhood for a child's frustration with parental limits to erupt into a tantrum. As two pediatricians write, "Almost all youngsters have these episodes occasionally, especially around ages two and three."[1] And it is a normal part of the growth for teenagers to occasionally lie for the sake of freedom. As one authority on adolescence observes, "It is, simply, unreasonable to expect adolescents always to tell you the truth. . . . They will tell you the truth or not as they see fit."[2] Responsible parents, however, are part of this developmental process, and they cannot surrender their oversight of the choices the child makes. *Just because a growth change is normal does not make the behaviors that go with it constructive, healthy, or right.* Thus the child is not allowed to use temper to manipulate his parents any more than the teenager is allowed to get away with lying. Distinguishing between *process* and *choice* is one of the trickiest tasks of parenting.

CONFLICTS OVER
A CHILD'S GROWTH

Growing up requires giving up, and the process can be painful for a child. Every developmental gain involves some kind of loss. Just as the infant gives up the breast for the bottle and the toddler gives up the bottle for the cup, so every step a child takes toward independence is a step away from the dependence he enjoyed before. There are rewards to growth: more competence and independence, increased social standing and approval in parents' eyes. As he takes his first steps, as he utters his first words, as he sings his first song, both he and his parents take pride in the accomplishment. Relinquished comforts are missed, however.

The growing child associates them with a simpler time of life. A preadolescent child can get angry seeing a parent cuddle a much younger sibling, jealous of the physical affection that he misses but can no longer comfortably accept. "Why don't you stop spoiling her!" he protests. "Put her down!" Some inappropriate teasing may occur when the older sibling takes out this resentment on a younger brother or sister. It helps if parents react with understanding. They can explain this hard part of growing up, "Just because we take less care of you as you grow older, that doesn't mean we care about you any less. We love you as much as ever, and we respect you even more." Then she pats her son on the shoulder, substituting the affectionate touch for the hug he will no longer accept.

Parental criticism can make enduring the loss from growth even harder, so parents should not act impatiently with their child for saying that he misses old indulgences: "I wish I hadn't grown too big for you to carry!" Nor should parents get angry when their child regresses to reclaim old consolations that have been given up: "Read me to sleep like you did when I was younger and feeling sick."

Remember that growing up is a clumsy dance, two steps forward and one step back, an alternating mix of progress and regress. Parents who become impatient with this inconsistency or who choose to punish the child for falling back add disapproval to an inherently risky process. An anxious child who feels stressed, for example, may regress to earlier behavior to get parents to offer a familiar comforting response, becoming clingy. A toilet-trained child may begin to wet himself again, anything to reclaim the former sense of security that he had when he was so closely held and cared for. For some parents, such acts of regression are infuriating because they want to be liberated from a child's dependency. They may end up discouraging the progress they want: "Stop acting like a baby!" "Why don't you grow up?" "Act your age!" These are expressions of parental impatience with normal regression, but they can be fighting words to the child. In a mutually unhappy way, the child may use conflict to keep the parent close and involved during an insecure time.

UNDERSTANDING THE GROWTH
CHANGES OF CHILDHOOD

It takes two acts of courage to grow. Enduring loss of some old comfort is one; facing parental impatience and insensitivity to new development is the other. Trying to keep pace with their child's changes can be confusing for parents. Playing catch-up is often the best they can do. Whether it's in the transition out of childhood into early adolescence, or from the "wonderful ones" to the "terrible twos," parenting never stays the same. A child is constantly changing, and when parents feel they have their child figured out, he or she becomes different to live with. It can help ease adjustment to their child's development for parents to identify her motivation and objective in growing through these changes. Dissatisfied with some aspect of her current level of functioning, she wants to do more with and for herself. When she does, there comes an increased sense of competence and independence, the twin objectives that drive all childhood growth. How do parents know when she is ready to grow? When she feels that readiness within herself and when, through her words and actions, she makes her determination clear. For example, consider the child who decides it is time to dress herself. "I can do it!" she impatiently announces to her parents. *Letting go is one way parents help their child grow.*

Parents need to treat developmental changes as a normal part of growing up and not misinterpret them as willful opposition. Change may involve oppositional behavior, but the child is marching to the drum of internal growth. These experiences of change are transformative. Consider the questions that arise around three momentous developmental changes that parents need both to celebrate and to help the child to manage.

- Able to crawl and then to walk, how is the child to manage *physical mobility*? Can she go anywhere she wants?
- Able to learn language and to talk, how is the child to manage *verbal fluency*? Can she say whatever she wants?
- Able to relate to others and to play, how is she to manage *social companionship*? Can she treat other people any way she wants?

The child may make choices in each change that parents cannot approve, whether it's running across the street, not telling them the truth, or hitting friends who won't agree. These are not times to engage in conflict; these are times to educate the child through direction and redirection, in each case helping the child *channel* a new kind of freedom in a safe, constructive, and healthy way. The mantra for parents at these times is, "This is what you can do differently instead."

UNDERSTANDING THE GROWTH CHANGES OF ADOLESCENCE

During adolescence, the young person begins to separate from his or her childhood self so that the journey to manhood or womanhood can begin. The adolescent tries on a host of new identities, friend-ships, interests, and cultural identifications, becoming a vortex of change in the family to which many parents struggle to adjust.

What makes this change difficult for the adolescent to manage and for his parents to understand is his own *ambivalence* toward the transformation that is now underway. Caught between feelings of loss and fear, adolescents often experience an emotional tug-of-war within themselves. Feeling honestly conflicted about the change that they both want and don't want, teenagers send mixed messages. Consider just a few typical contradictory statements most parents hear daily.

- "Tell me what to do!"/"Don't tell me what to do!"
- "Do it for me!"/"Let me do it!"
- "Leave me alone!"/"Pay attention to me!"
- "Stop asking so many questions!"/"Show some interest in me!"
- "I'm not going!"/"Take me along!"
- "I don't want to know!"/"Tell me what's going on!"

Which way does the adolescent want it? The answer is both ways. Parents need not fight for consistency; they should get used to the push and pull of two powerful sets of emotions. And they should be sensitive to the fact that their adolescent is not only changing in ways that cause conflicts with them, but may be doing the same with long-standing friends.

One particularly difficult set of growth conflicts that often occur during this transition has to do with the loss of childhood friendships. Best friends who shared a connection that was so close it sometimes seemed that they were the same person, knowing each other's thoughts without having to be told, often grow apart. One of them develops different interests and is drawn to new friends, and their old intimacy and compatibility no longer bind them together. The friend who pulls away often feels guilty, while the one left behind feels rejected. The growing separation between them is marked by painful conflict as one pursues a new direction and the other fights to hold on to what they had, but the old best friendship between them is irretrievably lost.

The parental role in this situation is to help their child understand that late elementary school and middle school are periods of great personal change and redefinition for everyone. They can explain that when best friends don't get along anymore, it is nobody's fault; it is not a matter of anyone being mean. It is, however, natural for the friend who was left behind to feel bereft, as though part of herself has been torn away. Parental understanding and companionship at this time are important safeguards against a child's despondency. Underneath the child's anger is a well of pain that she needs to talk about so that she does not interpret the rejection as a sign of her worthlessness. Parental support during this hard time can help the lonely child withstand her loss until she makes new friendships.

Just as such shifting social alliances can feel like betrayal to the friend left behind, parents often view their teenager's new persona as a betrayal of them. Parents who grew up poor and became well-off through hard work, for example, may feel offended by free-spending adolescents who take their financial comfort for granted. The parents might complain, "We grew up knowing the value of the hard-earned dollar, but our kids act like having money to spend is no big deal. Kids these days are spoiled!" In one such family, the parents are truly conflicted. They want to give their children all the advantages they didn't have, but they resent them for having it easy. They don't want their children to struggle for economic survival, but they do want them to appreciate the good fortune of growing up without the privations they knew. Some degree of cultural gap is inevitable between parent and child, and it becomes most apparent in adolescence because social and cultural changes from one generation to another always create this contrast. The major growth change in adolescence is not simply social; it is also chemical and physiological. With the onset of puberty and the arrival of sexual maturity, conflicts over sexual role changes begin.

SEX-ROLE CONFLICTS

Conflicts with parents may become especially pronounced as the teenager undergoes a complicated redefinition as a sexual being. Now the son no longer wants to be a child; he wants to grow into a man like his father. Now the girl no longer wants to be a child; she wants to grow into a woman like her mother. But how much to model after this same-sex parent? that is one question. And what about relating to the parent of the other sex? The conflict issues vary depending on the sex of the parent and the sex of the adolescent involved.

Conflict between adolescents and their mothers often stems from feeling *too close to her for comfort.* I believe the son fights with his mother to put distance between them because of an underlying fear that being too close to his mother will diminish his maleness at a time when he is trying to differentiate himself from both his parents. He also wants to stand up as a man to her authority and often becomes more argumentative. The daughter fights with her mother too, but her motivations are mixed. She wants to disconnect from her in order to gain independence. At the same time, she wants to stay connected, fearing a loss of the bond between them. Because the teenage daughter wants separation and closeness, differentiation from and similarity to her mother, conflicts between them can be particularly intense.

Conflicts between adolescents and their fathers often stem from feeling *too different for his approval.* The son fights with his father to get respect and the affirmation of being treated like his own man. Wanting to resemble his dad, the boy is also driven by the fear of not measuring up to him. The daughter fights with her father to gain appreciation and affirmation because she fears estrangement from him, that he won't value her or take her seriously because she is not male.

As a parent, if you sense that any of these issues are behind your conflict with your teenager, you might consider making the following statements, *but only if* you truly mean them:

- A mother might say to her teenager daughter, "No matter how different we are as women, we will always love and appreciate our differences and stay connected that way."
- A mother might say to her teenage son, "The fact that we spend less time together does not mean we love each other less. It means this is a time for you to have room to grow into the man you will become."

- A father might say to a teenage son, "What I wish for you is not that you copy me or follow my path in life, but be true to yourself and discover the man you want to be."
- A father might say to his teenage daughter, "I will always value the human being that you are, respect the woman you are becoming, and remain your biggest fan."

Part of a mother's "developmental task" during this period is to learn to surrender control, to give her teenage children love and the space they need to grow. Part of a father's developmental task is to learn to reach out to his teenagers with the gift of understanding and his ongoing acceptance. The parenting framework changes, but parental responsibilities do not diminish.

WRITING THE FREEDOM CONTRACT

What the adolescent wants most is more freedom. Parents want to give it to him, but they are obliged to do some hard bargaining to make sure he earns it by behaving responsibly. Why is responsibility important? Because with every increase in freedom comes an increased *risk* of possible harm. Only increased capacity for responsibility can regulate that risk. So parents only allow their sixteen-year-old the risk of getting behind the wheel of a car when they feel assured that he is responsible enough not to mix drinking or drugging with driving.

Bargaining usually entails some conflict, since how much freedom and how much responsibility are often a source of disagreement between parent and teenager. Parents should take the initiative in this discussion by explaining to their teenager, "For you to get the freedoms you want from us, here are six kinds of responsibilities that we need from you." Then parents can proceed to lay out what I call "The Freedom Contract." The provisions are as follows.

- TRUTH: "You will keep us reliably informed with adequate and accurate information about what is happening in your life and your plans."
- CONTRIBUTION: "You will live in a mutual relationship with us, doing for family in return for all that family does for you."

- COMMITMENT: "Your word will be good; you will keep the agreements and promises you make with us."
- MATURITY: "You will demonstrate socially appropriate behavior at home, at school, and out in the world."
- AVAILABILITY: "You will be open to talking with us about any concern we have at any time."
- COURTESY: "When we have something to discuss with you, or when we disagree, you will communicate to us with the same respect we do with you."

When your sixteen-year-old asks you whether she can go to a late movie with friends, review together how well she lived up to the freedom contract the last time she asked for a new privilege. If she held up her end of the bargain, work out the terms of the new permission. If not, discuss where she has been falling short and the changes you need to see before you can grant her request. You want evidence that she is able to accept greater responsibility. You cannot bargain based on her reassuring words or promises to "do better" next time. In addition to using the freedom contract to clarify the understanding between them and their teenager, parents also have to take responsibility for the expectations of the teenager that set.

MANAGING EXPECTATIONS

The developmental changes of their son or daughter's adolescence tend to be more challenging for parents than the changes in earlier childhood because the teenager has a more powerful agenda for independence than the child. Parental authority that the child tended to accept, the adolescent increasingly contests. This is as it should be. His job is to push for more room to grow just as his parents' job is to resist this push with appropriate demands for responsibility. To moderate the frequency and intensity of this conflict and not overreact to it, *parents must set realistic expectations to anticipate normal changes that accompany adolescent growth.* So it is important that parents understand what expectations are and how they function.

Expectations are just mental sets that people use to anticipate change so they do not have to proceed through life in utter ignorance about the future. Our expectations help prepare us for what is going to happen next. We have expectations about what we think *will happen* (predictions), what we *want to have happen* (ambitions), and what we *believe should happen* (conditions). Here are three parental expectations you might have for your child:

- Your *prediction* is that he will keep you adequately informed about what he is doing.
- Your *ambition* is that he will continue to want to work hard to do well at school.
- Your *condition* is that as a member of the family he should promptly help when you ask him to do something.

Mental sets have emotional consequences: To the degree your child keeps you adequately informed, you feel secure because he fulfilled your prediction. To the degree he keeps up his grades, you feel satisfied because your ambition has been fulfilled. To the degree he willingly lends a hand when you ask him to, you feel in charge because he met your condition. What you expect is what you get. But what happens in adolescence, when these old expectations may no longer fit his changed behavior?

Now he sometimes violates your prediction that he will keep you informed, telling you less than you need to know, and you feel anxious. Now, he sometimes violates your ambition that he will perform well in school by placing more importance on making friends than making grades, and you feel disappointed and sad. Now he sometimes violates your condition that he should readily help out when needed by making empty promises or delays, and you feel betrayed and angry. Not anticipating these common adolescent changes, you are at risk of overreacting, making a parenting challenge even more difficult.

This is not to say that what you *expect* you should also *accept*. Responsible parents should *not* turn a blind eye to noncommunication, flagging effort at school, and unwillingness to contribute household help. However, by anticipating these changes with a realistic set of expectations, parents can reduce the potential that they will feel surprised, disappointed, or betrayed when they occur. Such misguided parental reactions can incite a heated conflict when the situation calls for serious discussion.

Here are some common problematic changes to anticipate as your child grows his way through the four stages of adolescence:

- In *early adolescence* (ages nine to thirteen) expect negativity in the form of complaints, active and passive resistance (argument and delay), and testing of limits (seeing what behaviors he can get away with, for example, making prank calls, vandalizing, and shoplifting).
- In *mid-adolescence* (ages thirteen to fifteen) expect a harder push for social freedom (hanging out at the mall), more lying about doing the forbidden (sneaking out), and increased peer pressure to take risks (experimenting with alcohol or drugs).
- In *late adolescence* (ages fifteen to eighteen) expect more interest in "acting grown-up" (dating and driving), emotional and often sexual involvement in romantic relationships, and more recreational use of alcohol or drugs at parties.
- In the trial independence stage of *early adulthood* (ages eighteen to twenty-three) expect crises about managing commitments like credit and job obligations, more confusion about direction in life like deciding on a career, and more distraction from a cohort of peers who are also breaking commitments and undirected, frequently partying to delay or escape adult responsibility.

If parents know what to expect, they are less like to emotionally overreact when problematic adolescent changes occur.

Finally, parents can anticipate that the focus of conflict will change through these four stages of adolescent growth.

- *Early adolescence* (ages nine to thirteen). Heightened sensitivity to unfairness: "What right do you have to tell me what I must and cannot do?"
- *Mid-adolescence* (ages thirteen to fifteen). Heightened peer pressure and social urgency: "My life will be ruined if you don't let me go to the party!"

- *Late adolescence* (ages fifteen to eighteen). *Heightened impatience to self-regulate*: "I'll be gone in a year, so I should be able to set my own hours."
- *Early adulthood* (ages eighteen to twenty-three). Heightened need for the appearance of adult self-sufficiency: "Just pay my expenses and let me lead my own life!"

Adolescent conflict lasts until true independence is declared, which today can be into the mid-twenties or later.

More social freedom is not the only thing the adolescent is after; it behooves parents to factor in the huge *technological change* in the context of which all adolescents live, the Internet. Now issues about permissible freedom become enormously complex. Parents must take stands for responsible Internet use and be prepared to engage in conflict in their defense.

A WORD ABOUT THE INTERNET

Come adolescence, young people lead a *double life.* The first life is the one that parents are told about and can observe. The second life is the one that parents are not told about and do not see. It is this deliberately hidden second life that the Internet wildly expands. Think about it. The Internet is not a discrete world with clear boundaries and a well-mapped cartography. It is an infinite universe of continually evolving content and interactive applications. In 2006, it was reported that the number of web sites with a domain name and content had grown from 18,000 in 1995 to over 100 million at the date the story was written.[3]

Even the most technologically sophisticated of us are ignorant of most of what is out there now. In 1990, the online world may have been mostly peripheral to children's lives; by 2000, it had become a parallel universe competing for their attention; and today it is the primary world for many children who spend most of their recreational hours online. The information and opportunities for interaction offered on the Internet are staggering, and so is the ease with which they can be accessed. *Your child doesn't have to physically go anywhere to go everywhere.*

You know he is safe at home in the real world, but you may have no idea where he is in the virtual world of the Internet.

Part of a parent's job is to supervise a growing child's freedom so risk is moderated while responsibility is learned. Freedom on the Internet is no exception to this rule. And as with other issues of freedom, parent and child come into conflict over the setting and patrolling of safe boundaries. Parents need to be in regular dialogue with a child about the Internet. If you don't find yourself in disagreement with your child over his online use, you are probably not doing an adequate job of supervision. You must ask yourself some elementary questions about your child's online use, because her safety and well-being are at stake.

- WHY do you want your child using the Internet at all? The answer may be educational: to acquire experience, knowledge, and skills. She will need those skills to navigate her way through the real world as an adult. *Your job is to supervise the online training your child gets at home.*
- WHERE do you want/not want your child to go in the vast Internet world? What sites do you *not* want your child to visit? Hate, gambling, drug, violence, dating, sex sites, or what? *Your job is to supervise where your child gets to go in the online world.*
- WHAT Internet content do you not want your child bringing into your lives, into the lives of younger siblings? And what representation do you want your child communicating and posting about him/herself in that world? Is misrepresentation of age okay with you? *Your job is to supervise what comes in and what goes up online.*
- WHOM do you want your child interacting with on the Internet? Do you want your child interacting with strangers? In what context is this okay? Do you want your child giving or receiving online mistreatment like bullying or rumor mongering with friends? *Your job is to supervise your child's Internet relationships and how they are conducted.*
- HOW MUCH online privacy do you want to give your child, how much communication about her Internet experience do you expect, and how much exposure to Internet stimulation do you want to allow? *Your job is to supervise the amount of online activity so it does not become secretive, entrapping, or overwhelming.*

- WHERE in the house do you want to put your computer? To which online services do you want to subscribe? The more privately your child's computer is placed, the more potential for online abuse occurs. *Your job is to supervise how publicly (family room) or privately (child's bedroom) the computer is placed in your home, and what kinds of online media, gaming, and other services are available to your child.*

- HOW MUCH is too much time for your child to spend on the Internet? Is she throwing her life out of healthy balance? Online time is indoor, sedentary, isolated, and often fantasy-based; time spent outdoors is physically active, socially interactive, and engaging with real-world challenges. *Your job is to supervise how much of your child's time is spent on the Internet, and how much time is spent on real-world skill development and physical activity.*

If you are thinking of giving your child a wireless laptop computer or a hand-held computing device with Internet access, ask yourself: "How are we going to adequately monitor this additional opportunity for use?"

Parents need to keep fighting to get children, particularly adolescents, to respect the risks of online activity, when they may be unwilling to acknowledge any risk at all.

Why can't the teenager see the possible dangers you are talking about? The answer is *denial*. Adolescence is the age of adventure. Discovering and experimenting with the adult world is a major motivation in adolescence, and the Internet is a great repository of all things forbidden. Of course, growing up is always fraught with risks as teenagers are compelled to seek out new experiences. To deal with her fears, which might prevent the trying, the adolescent engages in denial, resorting to cavalier statements: "It's not going to happen to me! I'm too smart to fall for that! I know all about that!"

Parents must understand that their teenager can't grow and change without taking risks and can't take risks without denying vulnerability. In the face of this denial and despite their teenager's objections, parents need to keep reminding her of the basic risks of online activity. The key to effective communication here is not arguing to defend your point of view; it is explaining, "I am telling you this to inform your choice, not to change your mind."

Here are just a few online risks parents might want to point out to a child.

- You are never just a spectator on the Internet. You are always a participant. You watch TV, but you enter the Internet. Cyberspace is dwelling space. Online, you are not invisible, you are identifiable. You are a presence and a destination. Wherever you link can link back to you. *You always run the risk of reciprocity.*

- You have no privacy on the Internet. Everything is public. Whatever you send goes you know not where and can be observed by you know not who. With every click you sacrifice one more increment of personal privacy. You leave an electronic trail of your online activity behind. You give up far more freedom than you get. *You always run the risk of exposure.*

- You have no power to retract, erase, or otherwise destroy any movements you made or messages you sent on the Internet. Nothing is destroyed. Data is simply moved or rearranged. There is no deletion, only disintegration, of data (which can be recompiled). Every action you take online adds to your historical record of online activities. Internet activity is additive. There is no subtraction. *You always run the risk of permanency.*

- You get nothing for free when you use the Internet. Even when you are not deliberately paying for what you see or want, you are still paying a price for participating online. You are becoming part of a vast market system in which players unknown to you are out to make some kind of direct or indirect profit off what is known about you. Your personal information is stored and sold for somebody's advantage. *You always run the risk of commercial exploitation.*

- You may believe that what you read and see and hear online is real and true, but it is all to some degree virtual and made up. The most well-crafted and convincing web sites that are supposed to look official, authoritative, honest, and authentic can be filled with misinformation. The Internet is filled with deliberate misrepresentation. *You always run the risk of deception.*

- You may feel safe in your home playing on a computer, but as soon as you go online you are playing far away from home in an unimaginably vast universe. There are all manner of dangers from malcontents out to get you. When you go on the Internet you can be delivered to strangers who are predators. The more you share about yourself, the more your vulnerability increases. *You always run the risk of victimization.*

- You enter the Internet more than once for any reason and that repetition, repeated many times over, can become automatic. Without thinking you go online again simply because it is now familiar, because you have done it before. Soon it becomes a regular part of your routine that you depend upon to mark your day and fill your time. *You always run the risk of habituation.*

- You interact through email or instant messaging and the experience seems sociable as you keep in touch. However, without you or other parties physically interacting, it can become your primary and preferred way to communicate, and then this exchange can become *asocial.* The social cues observed and experienced in actual in-person contact are missing when communication is mediated online. People start to feel less connected because they are not talking face to face. *There is always the risk of isolation.*

Parents have the responsibility to discuss with their children the real risks of participating in this virtual world.

The Internet offers many wonderful things. It is an exciting electronic frontier, an encyclopedia of life, a source of communication and creative expression. It offers an infinite source of entertainment and escape, and is a universal marketplace. It has become an essential educational and business tool. It is a social necessity, the new "street corner," particularly for adolescents, a meeting place to hang out with friends and discover new relationships.

The Internet has a shaping effect on children as they grow. Years hence, the evolutionary impact of this extraordinary technology will become clearer. Based on my admittedly limited observation, I believe the psychological effect of the Internet might include some of the following:

- more divided attention and a shorter attention span,

- more impatience and a greater need for immediate gratification,
- more need for stimulation to capture and hold a child's interest,
- more reliance on electronically mediated, fragmentary communication,
- more need to be present and socially connected in the virtual world,
- less live, face-to-face social contact and less sensitivity to social and emotional cues,
- less comfort with emotional intimacy and making empathetic connections,
- less tolerance for solitude, silence, stillness, and quiet reflection,
- less time spent communicating and connecting with family,
- less capacity to distinguish between the worlds of virtual and actual experience,
- less sensitivity to sensational images from fantasy computer games (desensitization).

It is part of the parent's job to figure out what constitutes healthy Internet use with each child. To prevent unnecessary conflict with your child over online experience, practice prevention. Set up ground rules and talk about possible issues *before* they become sources of disagreement. By the onset of adolescence (ages nine to thirteen) when the child becomes more curious about and more adventurous in the grown-up world, you should have *specified, reviewed*, and *ratified* the conditions for traveling the Internet. (This is no different from what you will do later with another significant freedom, driving a car, where you do not give your child permission to "go anywhere you want or do anything you want whenever you want." You set destination limits and maybe spot-check the fuel gauge, odometer, or GPS system.) You have specified answers to the questions such as where your child can go and what he can do, and you have reviewed major risks. You have ratified a "joint-company agreement" with your child in which you say, "Where you are free to go, I expect to be free to go as well." You are not saying you are going to monitor his every moment on the Internet, but you are saying that just as you routinely check the computer for adware, spyware, and viruses, you will also be *spot-checking* your child's online activities to make sure they stay within approved, safe, and healthy bounds. And should you have any questions, you expect a forthright discussion and explanation. Your child must live with the uncertainty of not knowing when you check the computer or what you know, because your checking is unpredictable. This uncertainty has some cautionary power. There should be an agreement about passwords: you expect to be informed of passwords he uses so you are not locked out of any place he goes, in the same way your child is allowed no private (secret) email addresses or web pages. If your child wants online freedom, then he must agree to hold to a responsible online account.

If you say, as some parents do, "But I am a computer illiterate!" then educate yourself about this huge technological change so you can monitor what is going on. Just because your child is more practiced on the Internet doesn't mean you cannot learn enough to provide adequate supervision. That is your responsibility. It does neither parent nor child any good for the adult to act clueless and helpless. Parents must be able and willing to do regular supervision, to risk responsible conflict with their child. Communicate permissible freedom and acceptable risk so that he or she learns to navigate, to evaluate, to interact, and to educate in the safe and constructive use of the Internet. As one writer put it: "Some [parents] will say you should simply trust your child, that if he is old enough to go on the Internet he is old enough to know the dangers. Trust is one thing, but surrendering parental responsibility to a machine that allows the entire world access to your home borders on negligence."[4] *In addition, parents must fight to keep a child's online activities from taking precedence over important occasions for parent and child to communicate and for family time together.*

THREE IDEAS ABOUT
CHANGE AND CONFLICT
TO CARRY FORWARD

- The demands for change in families cause conflict when one party pushes for *new* experience (often the growing child) and the other party (often the parents) insist on defending the *old* order, creating increasing intergenerational conflicts over freedom, particularly during the adolescent years.

- By keeping their expectations current with the changing reality of their child's development, parents can avoid overreacting emotionally in conflict when new growth occurs.
- When a child opposes a family change, rather than fight against his resistance and create a conflict, parents can help the child strategize how best to manage this unwelcome turn of events.

7

AUTHORITY AND CONFLICT

Simply defined, *personal power is the capacity to get one's way*—with oneself (through self-control), with other people (through influence), and out in the world (through determination). Because of their caretaking responsibility, most parents want sufficient personal power over their children to influence their behavior; hence they assume a right of *adult authority* that they want respected. But pulling rank on a child is not as simple as it seems. *The responsible assertion of parental authority will sometimes engender conflict between parents and the growing child. That's just how it works.*

PARENTAL CONTROL

Parents assume authority to place themselves in a position of power over a child in order to direct his or her behavior. However, this may not work with a strong-willed child or an adolescent. The only part of the demand ("Now!") or denial ("No!") that this child refuses to understand is "Why?" and so a parental order or a prohibition can spur argument in response. In the words of one parent, "When I say 'no,' my four-year-old hears a call to war!"

Of course, parents' belief that they can actually control their child is an illusion, albeit one they dearly wish were true. For example, the infant is crying, so the father picks her up, rocks her gently, speaks to her in soothing tones, and she soon quiets down. "I made her stop crying," thinks the man. No, he didn't. He has no control over the child's crying. Only the child does. But the dad likes to think he possesses consoling power. In fact, the man tried certain methods meant to be consoling and then the child in some primitive way *decided*, for unknown causes the father will never know, to stop crying. At age two, the same child is testing her power with a defiant "No!" at every turn. Her father uses his larger physical size, commanding words ("You will!"), and loud tone of voice to gain the stubborn child's compliance. He again believes that he has "made her behave" the way he wants. Why did the child give into him on this occasion? It was not because he was able to force her behavior. For whatever reason, she *chose* to go along.

I believe the power of parental authority comes down to eight points.

- The initial function of parental authority is to set and supervise a system of family rules and restraints that encourage the child along a path of safe and healthy growth.
- Compliance with this system depends *not* on parental control but on the child's *choice* to ignore, oppose, or cooperate with what parents want, thus the formula: *command + consent = compliance*.
- Parents do have power over their own choices, and in this way they can influence the child's decision to comply.
- To get the child to give consent, parents must *convince* her to cooperate.
- If the child refuses to comply, the job of parents is to keep creating the opportunity for cooperative choice, either by repeating the choice they tried before or by generating a different one.
- In parent/child conflict, the more persistent party, or the one who generates the most alternative choices for resolving it, is usually the party that prevails.
- Parents who give up, get mad, or try to force compliance are usually less influential than parents who calmly persist and keep generating choices.
- The ultimate goal of parental authority is to teach the child sufficient responsibility, self-regulation, and autonomy that he can assume effective governing authority over his own life as an adult.

Sometimes a young child defies parental control.

- "You can't stop me!"
- "You can't make me!"
- "I don't have to do what you say!"
- "It's my life, and I will do what I want!"

In the face of such defiance, parents should *not* argue to defend their authority. Instead, they should take the issue off the table by agreeing. They can say something like, "Who controls your choices is not worth arguing about. You do. That's how it works. We make choices about what we want you to do. You make choices to do or not do what we want. And then we make choices about consequences for your decisions—choices you like when you have done what we asked, choices you don't like when you have not. In this sense, you have the power to influence our choices with your own." Parents who get into arguments about control with a child are engaging in a senseless debate. Their time is better spent strategizing to gain influence and consent.

Parents should explain to the young child, and repeat with the adolescent, why their authority is necessary, perhaps saying something like: "It is our job to protect you, keep you safe, and prepare you to act as an adult. As long as you live with us, we are responsible for your care. This means that we will sometimes be taking stands against what you want for reasons we believe are in your best interests. There will be conflict between us as a result. Sometimes our job is to make demands, set limits, ask questions, challenge or confront you, and apply consequences. When we are doing our parenting job, you may think we are being mean, insensitive, or unfair. What I want you to know is that even though it may sometimes feel like we are the enemy, we are always your friends. Using our authority to oppose you is one of the hardest parts of our parenting job, particularly when you believe we are using it *against* you. Please remember that we are always on your side." The beneficial, shaping role of parental authority, however, can be hard for a child to understand, at least at the time.

Consider the family out for a fast-food supper—Mom, Dad, and the three kids. The mother, according to family custom, declares: "Before we eat, let's say Grace." But the youngest child, age four, objects. "I don't want to say Grace, I want to eat. I'm not going to say Grace!" But everybody else does, and when they are finished, the mother carefully removes the hamburger from the four-year-old's plate without saying a word. "I'm hungry," he protests, as the others eat and ignore him. Finally, he tugs on his mother's arm. "I want to say Grace," he whispers. "All right," she agrees, and the family stops eating and says Grace again. Then the mother puts the hamburger back on the child's plate. The child begins to eat, but more important, according to both parents, he never questions the custom of family prayer at mealtime again. Even a very young child will challenge parental authority, but by quietly holding firm, these parents allowed the child to choose to comply.

Parental influence is all the "power" parents have, and used judiciously, it usually proves to be enough because it can be exercised in multiple ways. Parents assert influence by the *example they model* (who and how they are), by the *treatment they give* (how they choose to act and react with the child), by the *family structure they impose* (what they value and allow), and by the *education they impart* (information and instruction they provide).

ASSERTING AUTHORITY

Until the young person gathers enough understanding, experience, and responsibility to function independently, parents are the rule makers. Living on parental terms can be frustrating for a child when parents enforce rules for her that they are free to ignore. She may resent the inequity of what she perceives as a double standard in the family: "Why do I have to go to bed early when you don't?" However, a family is *not* a democratic system with voting power shared equally, where children are given comparable standing and voice to the adults. A child's growth is a gathering of power, from dependence to independence, continually contesting the restraints and demands parents impose to create more room to grow. *A healthy child pushes for all the freedom she can get, as soon as she can get it. Responsible parents restrain that push within the interests of safety and responsibility.* This built-in opposition creates endless opportunities for conflict. I do not believe that there has ever been or will ever be a child who has not tested parental authority to some degree, to see

- "Are parents really in charge?"
- "Do parents really mean what they say?"
- "Can parents really back up what they want?"

Sometimes parents will take the testing of their authority as a sign of disrespect. Nothing could be further from the truth. When a child contests parental authority it shows that she believes there is some superior standing there to be challenged. If you allow this challenge, but hold fast to your position, and the child goes along with your wishes, then she has respected your authority. If she has not used a respectful tone or language in the process of this challenge, then that is a secondary issue that needs attention because it bears on the conduct of conflict and how you want it to be done. Otherwise, she has made a face-saving compromise: She has her *say*, then she gives you your *way*. In general, the more willful the child or the more resistant the adolescent, the more this compromise is the price you must be willing to pay for receiving consent.

FIGHTING FOR AUTHORITY

So when is parental authority worth fighting for? The answer can be expressed in the *three Rs*: where matters of *risks*, *rules*, and *respect* are concerned. "We will not allow you to put your personal safety at *risk* by acting dangerously." So parents secure the child when crossing the street by having him hold their hand. "To get the freedoms you want you must obey the *rules* we set." So parents decree that weekday play with friends can begin only after homework is done. "To maintain good membership in this family, you must *respect* our household needs." So parents insist that after the child has made a snack he clean up the mess he has created.

These invocations of parental authority put the errant child on notice that here is an issue where parents are prepared to take a stand.

Parents may agree with the first two Rs, risk taking and rule keeping, but may question the importance of the third R, respect for family responsibilities. After all, by comparison to matters of personal safety and social obedience, preserving household order and contributing chores may seem like little things, too minor to be worth fighting about. In fact, I have heard many parents parrot that common piece of advice, "Don't sweat the small stuff." They wonder: "Should we keep after our child to clean up his room when it only leads to argument? Is it worth the constant conflict?" I believe the answer is "definitely yes," because *small things are really big things in disguise*. Here is why.

Little things such as not straightening the family room after play or not cleaning dishes he has dirtied can mask a larger issue; *specific acts often have symbolic meaning*. In this case, the larger issue at stake is represented by the question: "In this household, who is going to live on whose terms?" Are the parents going to live according to the disorder preferred by the child or is the child going to live according to the order that is comfortable for the parents? This is an authority issue that children keep probing as they grow.

Whenever a child doesn't put away his toys when he's finished playing with them, leaves the kitchen drawers and cupboards open or water running in the sink, or neglects to turn off the TV when no one is watching it, parents are put to "the test of terms." It is important for parents to address this behavior each time it occurs. When they do, they send a powerful message: "So long as you live in our home, you must abide by our household needs, and we will keep after you until you do." The worst response is for parents to do it themselves because it's "easier" than fighting with the child. It is not. The child gets out of doing the work, the parents send the message that they don't mean what they say, and the child feels that he doesn't have to pay attention to what he was told to do. Resentful, frustrated parents in this situation have to take some responsibility for the child's inaction because they have chosen not to follow through. Respect for the household needs of parents tends to get worse once the child enters adolescence. Maybe the child was content to confine personal disorder to his bedroom, but the adolescent wants to spread his disarray all over to stake a claim to the entire house. He scatters clothes and belongings and leftovers to mark his expanded territory to let his parents know that they have a larger person to contend with now. It is as if he is saying, "Make room for my presence everywhere!"

As parents, are you content to live in this teenager's expanded space? Perhaps not. This is why you insist that the adolescent respect your need for order that includes keeping things picked up, cleaned up, and put away because these household conditions are *symbolic of your authority*. In the home, you are in charge. This means that so long as he lives with you, dependent on your support, *he must live on your terms*.

In the very last stage of adolescence, trial independence (about ages eighteen to twenty-three), asserting this point can be taxing. When your twenty-one-year-old comes back home to live with you, perhaps because of flunking out of college or breaking off a relationship or losing a job, you can be thrown into similar conflicts. After she has been on her own, it can be very hard to go back to life on parental terms. When she cannot live within your household demands and restraints, you should *not* battle for control or try to change her ways. You need to respect her decision and calmly declare that since nothing less than living on her own terms is what she truly wants, you will need to set a time for her to leave and to live independently. Helping younger children to abide by parental terms at home is where parental discipline begins.

AUTHORITY AND DISCIPLINE

The purpose of discipline is to make demands and set limits that help the child learn to live according to family values and within family rules. From this training, the child acquires an ethical framework that shapes her moral outlook and develops habits of self-discipline that direct her personal conduct. Parents exercise much of their authority through discipline that even the most well-behaved children will occasionally ignore or oppose, creating conflict on that account.

Rather than be surprised or offended by these discipline problems, keep in mind the songwriter Billy Mutschler's line, which is true for both child and adult.

> "We're all just human beings,
> And now and then we step out of line."[1]

To a degree, all parental disciplinary rules are made to be occasionally broken. Parents discipline their children using a mix of instruction and correction, at best more instruction than correction. When correction becomes the rule, conflict tends to increase and discipline becomes harder to maintain because the relationship has become so negative and unrewarding for the child to live in. Excessive correction motivates him to become less cooperative and more resistant. Occasionally I try to explain this to the parent in counseling who complains, "No matter what consequence I apply, my child keeps misbehaving. Give me a punishment that will work!" At this point, there isn't one. Become over-reliant on correction and behavior problems tend to go from bad to worse. This is why parents must always maintain a sense of balance in their discipline: *The more negatively corrective they feel called upon to act, the more positively affirmative they must also find a way to be.*

Typically, parents rely on one or more of four strategies of discipline to get the child's cooperation. Each one exercises a different kind of influence to get the child's consent, and each one has the potential for inviting conflict. In brief, these strategies are as follows:

- *Guidance* has the power of persuasion. Parents tell the child what they expect him to do and why. Explaining the reason you are asking your child to do something tends to work better than making dictatorial demands. "We are having friends over tonight, so it would really be helpful to have your household chores done before they arrive." Guidance can lead to more conflict when parental explanation provokes an argument. Should this occur, listen to what is said, but stick to the reason that you gave for the request you made.

- *Supervision* has the power of pursuit. Parents repeat their request until the child complies, even if grudgingly. Persistence eventually wears down the child's resistance. "I intend to stay in this room until you're finished making your bed." Supervision can lead to more conflict when the pursuit or nagging provokes annoyance and complaint. Should this occur, listen to the complaint, but don't let the child's annoyance back you off.

- *Exchange points* have the power of provision. Parents withhold giving something the child wants until she has complied with what they asked her to do. "We are happy to let you go over to Jenny's house, but we need for you to finish cleaning up your room first." Exchange points can lead to more conflict when parental withholding provokes bargaining. Should this occur, listen to the child but then explain again that first the child must do for you before you do for her, holding fast to the condition you have set.

- *Structure* has the power of reward and punishment. Parents reward compliance with appreciation. "Thank you for getting home on time." They apply a negative consequence when the child fails to comply. "After sleeping over at a friend's and sneaking out, we will not let you stay there overnight for a while." Punishment can lead to more conflict when the child feels unjustly treated. Should the child accuse you of being unfair, listen to what is said, but stick to the consequence you have set for the violation that occurred.

If you still stick to your disciplinary guns after listening to the child's objections, the child may accuse you of *not* listening to her because you won't change your mind. At this point you may explain what listening is: "Listening means that I am paying attention to you and that I respect what you have to say. But listening doesn't necessarily mean that I agree or will go along with what I hear. I can disagree and refuse what you want, and still be listening to what you say."

While it is necessary to draw on your parental authority in order to impose appropriate discipline, the inappropriate use of authority can cause parental discipline to miscarry in four common ways:

1. *Relying on punishment as the discipline of first resort* when the child actively resists by arguing or passively resists by delaying. Punishment should not be used for minor irritations such as playing music too loud or neglecting to close the refrigerator door yet again. It should be reserved for major infractions like lying or stealing money from another family member. Punishment that feels unjust to a child because it is inappropriate injects more negative energy into the relationship. Remember the banking metaphor that is also the rule of cooperation with a child, and even more with a teenager: "No deposit, no return." The positive "deposits" of appreciation, approval, and affection from parents let him know that he mostly shines in your eyes and cause him to want to comply with your wishes. Because it is critical and aversive, punishment

should be administered selectively. As was mentioned earlier in this chapter and is worth repeating here, if it becomes the primary strategy a parent uses for discipline, then the child is given very little incentive to comply, and, in fact, has more incentive to resist. Punishing a child to improve his attitude usually has the opposite effect. Punishment is a corrective response to an intentional misbehavior, meant to discourage a repeat occurrence. It is *not* an appropriate response to a child's inadvertent transgressions. Punishing "crimes of ignorance," when what is needed is information, can generate conflict with a child who feels unfairly penalized. So the ten-year-old protests, "How was I to know I wasn't supposed to ride my bike over to my new friend's? You never told me, and now I'm grounded!" *Using criticism* is also an inappropriate use of punitive power. "You should be ashamed of yourself!" "You let us down!" "We're disappointed in you!" "You really did a dumb thing!" "You'll never learn!" These messages do not encourage compliance; they signal to a child that he has lost loving standing in his parents' eyes. They can generate hurt feelings and invite retaliation. Better to turn criticism into specific disagreement: "We really disagree with the choice you made, this is why, this is what we wish you had chosen to do differently, and this is what we need to have you do now."

2. *Getting into power struggles with a child* can cause a parent to use full force, verbally, emotionally, or physically, in order to prevail. When the child uses full force in response, one person's resistance is pitted against another's, to see who will yield first. Now an "isometric" encounter takes place. Isometric exercise develops strength through resistance. It is the practice of pushing against a stationary object to build muscle, and this is what the child in this scenario does. She pushes with all her might against the parent who is trying to force her to obey. Even when the child submits, she comes out stronger next time. Having built up her resistance "muscle," she is determined to push harder next time. Parents are better off not showing the child "who's boss." Instead, disengage from the child when opposition starts to build, then re-engage with the disciplinary issue when emotions have cooled down. Parents who cannot resist the temptation of fighting these battles for dominance often end up losing the war by training a more powerful adversary. Parental threats and acts of coercion intensify the child's feelings of hostility, particularly when used to force submission and to shut down the conflict.

3. *Inconsistently administering and enforcing rules* is the most common way parents undercut their authority. With all children, but particularly with a willful child or an adolescent, parental inconsistency sends a self-defeating double message: "Sometimes I really mean what I say and sometimes I don't." Few children can resist betting on "sometimes I don't." Hence the age-old parenting advice: Don't make any more rules than you can consistently patrol and don't make requests you are not prepared to pursue to completion. If you want your child to take you seriously, then be true to your word. Inconsistent discipline provokes conflict from a child who feels encouraged to keep testing rules to see whether this time you really mean what you say.

4. *Using physical punishment in lieu of words and reason can* discourage the child from using words and reason in return. Parents are most at risk of resorting to physical punishment when the child's wrong-doing has aroused their anger. When it comes to punishment, knowing what *not* to do is as important as knowing what to do. Don't punish your child in retaliation for feeling hurt, to even the score, to make her sorry by hurting her back, to show who is in charge, to ventilate your frustration, or to appease your anger. Although many parents would disagree with me, physical punishment is given more often to relieve parental frustration or anger than to discourage the child from repeating misbehavior. When parents poke, pinch, squeeze, pop, swat, spank, slap, or hit, they are only proving three things to the child. You are demonstrating that you are larger, more powerful, and feel entitled to be violent to get what you want or to stop what you don't want. Years later, when your child is grown-up, he or she may feel entitled to act the same way. In spanking, inflicting physical hurt can become the major message the child will remember, not the offense that punishment was intended to correct. As one thirteen-year-old bitterly put it after being physically disciplined by his dad, "He's not always going to be big enough to push me around!" All the arguments in support of spanking do not outweigh this one objection against it: Spanking teaches the child that using physical force is okay if you are bigger and stronger and cannot get what you want any other way. Simply put, *spanking shows that hitting is okay.*

A disciplinary decision that causes disunity between parents not only creates conflict in the marriage but invites the child to exploit the rift to his advantage. The child can pit one parent against the other—the strict, "mean" parent who never lets me have my way versus the permissive, "nice" parent who lets me do whatever I want.

The primary importance of a disciplinary decision is *not* whether it is effective with the child, but whether it is unifying for the parents and the authority they share. *Every disciplinary decision must be primarily for the sake of the marriage—parents "marrying" in agreement over how to instructionally or correctively respond to their child.* Going along with your partner's disciplinary authority when either one of you disagrees with the use of that disciplinary authority will weaken the marriage upon which the family welfare of children depends. You will be conducting parenting at the expense of partnership. Joint disciplinary decisions secure the child by supporting the marriage.

This does not mean that parents cannot agree to disagree, as when one parent says, "I don't think our child deserved to be sent to her room for a timeout for accidentally knocking the picture frame off the table and breaking it. But I will support your decision since I wasn't here. In return, I'd like us to talk about how I would have liked the incident handled differently so you can know where I stand."

As for disagreeing over what disciplinary response to make when in front of the child, there is nothing wrong in that so long as the child sees you both reasonably discuss and resolve the difference, coming together on a disciplinary decision you can both support. Now not only does the child see you present a "united front," she has seen you constructively work out a disagreement together, thus providing her with a living example of how conflict resolution is done. Discipline need not cause a lot of conflict between parents, and even between parents and child. At one parenting workshop, a father who had been an army captain testified to what he called "discipline without fighting." He and his wife had raised kids who most of the time did as they were asked. "What's your secret?" another parent wanted to know. The military man answered that there was no secret. The main thing was to make a system of rules that worked for him and his wife and that worked for the children so long as they worked with the system. "That's all there is to it."

Hearing this, one of the other parents grumbled, "Well you were probably just lucky to have obedient children," to which the military man laughingly agreed. "That's right, and just like the golfer said, the more we practiced, the *luckier* we got." I believe the military man was right in this: Children tend to be less prone to fight a system of family discipline where they know exactly what is consistently expected. This philosophy of authority is particularly useful when it comes to managing a major source of contention with children: the completion of homework.

HOMEWORK

It should come as no surprise that most children do not like doing homework. They have put in a full day in their classroom and they have to do homework at night. Will the school day never end?

Parents don't like policing the homework any more than the child likes doing it. However, most parents accept this onerous responsibility because neglected or incomplete homework lowers grades, affecting the child's educational opportunities later on.

The kind of parental authority that carries the day is not arguing, bargaining, rewarding, or punishing, but *consistent supervision*. It comes down to parents

- staying adequately informed about daily assignments,
- making sure that assignments and supporting materials are brought home,
- scheduling a regular time for homework to be accomplished,
- checking to make sure assignments are completed, and
- ensuring that completed assignments are faithfully turned in.

It is not unusual for parents to wonder who is really doing the homework. The unhappy answer is that both parent and child have a role. It requires the time and energy of them both, in partnership, to see that homework gets done every night.

Something that can be helpful for parents to keep in mind is that homework is not just about academic practice; it is also *training in a work ethic*. An important preparation for life is developing the self-discipline to do work one doesn't want to do. Parents do this every day, and homework allows children to learn how to do this every school night. Parents should do the supervision to support this unwelcome education. I believe it's a worthwhile investment of time and effort, albeit one their child will not thank them for at the time.

THE POWER OF "NO"

Probably no single word causes more conflict between parents and child than "no." From the child there is *resistance*, "No, I won't!" All the discipline strategies previously discussed provide approaches parents can use to overcome resistance and gain consent. From the parent there is *refusal*, "No, you can't!" Not all parental refusals, however, are the same. They vary in the intensity of conflict they can provoke. There is the *firm no* (the parent won't change her mind), the *questionable no* (the parent might change her mind), and the *reverse no* (the parent has changed her mind—from a yes to a no).

- The firm parental no can provoke the child to *complain*, "You never let me do anything!" Here the parent gets conflict in the form of *protest*.
- The questionable parental no can provoke the child, sensing parental uncertainty, to *argue*, "Before you decide, I have something to say." Here the parent gets conflict in the form of *debate*.
- The reverse parental no can provoke the child to *anger*, "You said I could and now you say I can't!" Here parents get conflict in the form of *outrage*.

How intense and wearing the conflict is can depend on the type of parental "no"—the firm no usually causing the least intensity, the reverse no generally causing the most.

Now consider what happens when parental authority demands excessive compliance or obedience. Fostering over-dependence often requires extreme conflict for the older adolescent to break free.

AUTHORITY ENCOURAGES DEPENDENCY

What happens when parents wield too much parental authority?

On the upside, an extreme statement of authority can create a conflict over dependency that an early adolescent uses to her advantage. Old enough to know that her parents can't actually stop her from doing anything (without her consent), the young person can feel frightened by this freedom because she still lacks the emotional maturity to handle it. In response to peer pressure to go along with some misadventure, she may not have the confidence to refuse and suffer the loss of social standing she imagines it would cost. Fortunately, her parents have given her a prohibition she can depend on, so she says, "My parents would punish me forever if I did that, so it's not worth it!" By blaming her parents, she gives herself an excuse not to participate and saves face in the bargain. The lesson for parents is this: *Don't be shy about using your authority to prohibit potentially dangerous behavior.* Let your child fight you but don't back off, because some time she may depend on your prohibitions to keep herself free from harm. Parental prohibitions can be used as ready-made excuses for staying out of trouble, particularly during the early and mid-adolescent years.

On the downside, extreme authority can foster a child's dependency, which is often expressed in two opposing characteristics—*submissiveness* and *rebellion.* The child who always does as he is told comes to rely on his parents to tell him what to do. The child who constantly refuses to do what she is told continually relies on her parents to determine what *not* to do. The rebellious child believes she is acting independently, but this is not so. By acting in opposition to what parents want, she is allowing her parents to define her behavior just as the submissive child does.

Parents can become enmeshed in a power struggle with a rebellious child, becoming increasingly negative and forceful with a child who often acts the same. Sometimes parents can minimize rebellion by giving the child more power of choice, offering not acceptance but the willingness to work with her in *accommodating* ways that still fulfill their request. So rather than fight the challenge to their authority, they offer some workable choices. In response to the refusal to pick up her room, they might say: "What would still work for us is for you to pick your clothes up off the floor and put them away where they belong now. You can make your bed later." Giving her a choice within their choice, they have accommodated her resistance and also defined for themselves an alternative, acceptable choice for compliance. Of course, they need to be sure that "later" the bed gets made as agreed.

The goal of growing up is for the young person to gather enough responsibility to become his own authority as an adult, finally depending upon himself to determine the course and conduct of his life. The more parents direct, dictate, and domineer, the more dependency they encourage. They can't have it both ways: wanting to remain in firm charge of what their child does and wanting him to develop independence at the same time.

If they want the child to learn more responsibility, parents have to risk letting go of some control, and this can be excruciatingly hard for parents who cannot bear to see their child fail or depart from their agenda. A high-achieving mother who was her high school valedictorian has similar ambitions for her son. She monitors and manages his school performance as she has done ever since his grades began to drop in middle school, believing that she is acting in his best interests and vowing to continue "until he shows me he has learned to organize and discipline himself and work up to capabilities." In response, her son is fighting *her* for autonomy and self-respect. She is afraid to let go for fear he won't try on his own, and he refuses to try until she lets go. A typical exchange between them in counseling sounded like this:

Mother: "You show me some responsibility and then I'll back off!"
Son: "Back off, and then I'll show some responsibility!"

The resolution of this conflict came at the end of junior year when the son made a declaration that his mother finally accepted: "The more you push me to do well, the less well I will do. If you really want me to care about my education, then it needs to be *my* priority, not yours. Maybe I'll study and work for me, but for sure I won't study and work for you."

Parents who demand obedience often find comfort in the illusion of being in control. Extremely authoritarian parents can produce a young person with little initiative or capacity to think for herself. Their strictness often begins to backfire on them when the child enters early adolescence. A child who cannot stand up to domineering parents, who passively obeys them at every turn, does not learn to share information about himself and work through differences. He often has a hard time refusing the demands of peers. He dependently obeys the governing power of the group just as he has always depended on the authority of his parents. Some parents in this situation will forbid a peer association in order to resolve the problem. In doing so, they encourage continued dependence, actually making the problem worse by enabling instead of teaching him to make his own decisions. A submissive child can become conflict averse, agreeing to things he knows he shouldn't do and doesn't want because he is afraid of the social consequences of saying "no."

In late adolescence, this submissive child may suddenly become very rebellious. What has happened? Often it is that she has begun to recognize how dependent she is. Seeing how much growth for independence she will need to cope with her approaching departure from home and parental care, she behaves extremely rebellious in order to sever the dependent tie. This passage can be difficult and painful unless her parents understand that *late-stage rebellion* is a sign that the time for more independence has arrived. Parents who remain convinced that their way is "the only way" may continue to micromanage the smallest details in the teenager's life. In response to a level of control that feels excessive to the historically submissive adolescent, enormous resentment builds in the child over time and finally explodes into serious conflict. As two researchers describe it, "Parents who derive major interpersonal benefits from the confiding, dependent behavior of their children may respond with bitter conflict when the adolescent attempts to gain a new kind of autonomy. Adolescents may have to rebel in extreme ways in order to establish some degree of independence. The transition from a parent-dominant to a more egalitarian hierarchy can provoke a serious crisis."[2]

LATE-STAGE REBELLION

Late-stage rebellion can be hard for parents because it happens suddenly. Overnight, it seems, their wonderful, pleasing child has become awful to live with. She fights them on the smallest requests and requirements, which represent the shackles of obedience she is now desperate to break. *For the child, the antidote to rebellion against parents is accepting the challenge for herself.* This means that the teenager needs to independently act *for* herself instead of dependently *against* them. Parents need to create opportunities for independence. For example, they can discuss letting her have the responsibility of doing her homework without nagging her about it, and to make her own social plans. Should she flounder at first in managing these responsibilities, as she likely will, they do not correct, criticize, or punish her. They let her make her own mistakes and figure out how to fix them because confidence in her own abilities is what she needs. She is no longer in the business of rebelliously *fighting* them; she is in the business of dealing with her own consequences and responsibly *righting* herself. And if she asks for their mentoring advice ("What should I do?"), they only offer it *after* she has thought through and come forward with a proposal of recovery for herself. *For parents, the constructive response to late-stage rebellion is not fighting to assert their authority, but respecting the teenager's readiness to assume more responsibility and letting go some control so she can have the opportunity to grow.*

The strategy here is to turn a potential conflict into a potential challenge. If parents want their late adolescent to act more maturely, the answer is not fighting with him to become that way. Instead, they need to turn over some of their responsibility for him, to him. Instead of meting out money as the need arises, for example, they can give him a fixed allotment to cover basic monthly expenses like school lunch, school supplies, clothing, entertainment, and car expenses if he drives. Then let him budget his outlay so that it lasts, and do not rescue him when it doesn't. Now parents are not in conflict with their teenager; he is in conflict with himself as he learns to manage more financial responsibility.

To forestall late stage rebellion and its desperate conflicts, parents can start testing the waters of *independent thinking* in their son or daughter as soon as adolescence gets underway in late elementary school and early middle school. Rather than automatically dictate what the child must do, they can say something like this: "Before I tell you what I would recommend, tell me what you think might be a way to go?" And if the parent thinks there is a reasonable chance that the teenager's suggestion might work, then say, "Okay, let's give your idea a try. If for some reason it doesn't work out, you can try something else." Not only is some independence transferred at this time; an important measure of respect is given.

Should the adolescent, flush with this sense of independence, demand, "Just let me be in charge of my own life," parents can explain what total independence requires. "If you really want full independence from us, you can have it. Just be sure you know what you are asking for. Total independence means moving out on your own, living on what you earn, and not relying on our support in any way." When the teenager replies that is not exactly what she meant, which was freedom without their interference while living at home, they can explain, "Then that means agreeing to still live on our terms."

Late-stage rebellion can generate particularly intense conflict in what I call a *collapsed adolescence*. When a young person delays the separation process because of parental dominance and her submissiveness, she may not begin adolescence until the middle of high school. This frequently happens with protected only children who have been tightly held by parents. It can be hard to let go of that security. Now, the first three stages of adolescence development suddenly "collapse" into a very intense period lasting about one-and-a-half to two years. The negative attitudes, increased resistance, and testing of limits that are the hallmarks of early adolescence overlap with the urgent desire for freedom, peer pressures, and push for independence of *mid-adolescence*, which in turn overlap with the even more urgent need for independence and to act more grown up that comes with late adolescence.

Parents in this situation face a tough challenge. They may need to impose restraints to slow growth down as they struggle to find a way to effectively communicate so their older teenager, who needs but may not want their advice, will listen to them. In other words, they must be calm, reasoned, and mature in conflict with a teenager who is often none of those things. If you are in this situation, re-read Chapter 2, "Emotion and Conflict," for what you must do to keep your "cool."

A collapsed adolescence that is delayed until after leaving home can be even more dramatic than one that happens when an adolescent is still living in the family. A young man who may have grown up in a military family or with severe religious training, or both, at last "liberates" himself at college by breaking *all* social restraints. In this case, parents do not attempt either to sanction or to "rescue" their son if he asks for help. They do, however, support him and offer advice if asked, affirming their confidence in him to solve his own problems and learn the life skills that hadn't been developed before. Henceforth, whatever conflicts arise, parents will *not* invoke their authority. They have let that go.

AUTHORITY AND COMMUNICATION

Social authority comes into play when one party is vested with superior power over another who is in a subordinate position. Whether represented by a police officer, a school principal, a boss, or a parent, all social authority rests on three rights in the relationship. Each one creates a different kind of a double standard, and each one poses a different kind of threat to the person in the subordinate position.

1. *Interrogation* is the right of authority to ask for information and expect answers. The inequity is "I have more right to know about you than you do about me." The threat is that *questions can be invasive of privacy.*
2. *Evaluation* is the right of authority to oversee and judge proper conduct. The inequity is "I have more right to review your behavior than you do to review mine." The threat is that *criticism can be accusatory.*
3. *Direction* is the right to order rule-abiding behavior and penalize infractions. The inequity is "I have more right to dictate what you do and what happens to you than you do with me." The threat is that *command can be coercive.*

The superior is always one up and the person in the subordinate position is always one down. Although the person in authority is vested with power over what happens to someone else and so can command obedience, she can also provoke distrust, fear, envy, or resentment in the person being told what to do. Correction by a social authority can cause one to feel vulnerable and on the defensive.

For example, just reflect on your experience when a police officer pulls you over, lights flashing in your rear-view mirror. Slowly she gets out of her car and walks up to your driver's side window while you carefully keep your hands in plain sight, gripping the wheel. You have been stopped by a social authority. She says:

- "Is there some reason you were driving so fast?" (Interrogation)
- "You were exceeding the safe speed limit." (Evaluation)
- "I'm going to issue you a ticket for speeding." (Direction)

Being corrected by a social authority, any child or adult can feel intimidated and anxious, or perhaps frustrated and angry if the encounter feels unfair. Because arguing can offend authority, speaking up is often sacrificed in order to prevent a bad situation from becoming worse. In conflict, authority wants to do the talking and doesn't want a lot of talking back, so equal exchange is not usually encouraged. In the case of a traffic stop, the officer's authority discourages two-way communication, which is okay since she and the detainee have no future relationship to be concerned about.

For a parent, however, the ongoing relationship with a recalcitrant child continues to matter. If the adult uses authority to shut down disagreement, he reduces the likelihood of open communication when the next point of difference arises. Now count the costs. He loses an opportunity to learn more about the child, and he prevents the child from practicing how to use conflict to increase understanding and create agreement between them.

Most important for a parent to remember is this: Whenever you invoke authority in conflict with your child, particularly in a forceful way, you emphasize the inequity of positional power between you, to significant psychological effect. At a workshop with police years ago, an officer succinctly summarized the authority she was empowered to administer to a citizen who refused to follow the law. "It's the same as being a parent with my kids," she explained. "If you won't stay in line, I have the power to frustrate your wants, limit your freedom, and even cause you some pain." That kind of authority sets up an opposition between her direct power as parent and the indirect power of her children that may have served her both well and badly. Having such direct power she could certainly manage her kids, but probably not as much as the children's indirect power allowed them to manipulate her. "Do you ever feel like your kids know how to maneuver you, more than you can maneuver them?" I asked. "Sure, all the time," she answered, then added perceptively: "That's 'cause they know me better than I know them." That is the price of forceful parental authority. To reduce the inequity of power between them and their parent, children gather indirect influence by observing that adult more closely than they are observed. In the process, they come to know that adult better than she knows them. Finally, they learn to use that knowledge and observation to play that adult in subtle ways most parents never fully appreciate or understand. An extremely authoritarian parent is usually unaware of how skillfully those he thinks he controls actually manage him. Fancying that he is in charge, he is usually blind to how the pretense, flattery, deceit, and token obedience of others keep him from seeing what is really going on, including the resentment that is building against him.

When in conflict with his child, a tired or stressed parent may be tempted to use his authority to resolve a disagreement quickly and efficiently: "Because I said so, that's why!" This can discourage two-way communication. At worst, as one psychologist observes, "a big power imbalance tends to invite abuse of some kind."[3] For example, there is the frustrated parent who can't stand any more fussing from the little child and resorts to yelling and threatening to shut the crying up. *When angry parents invoke authority to resolve a conflict, there is a higher likelihood some level of overreaction may follow.*

Getting from conflict to communication depends on whether parental authority is used coercively or collaboratively.

COERCIVE AND COLLABORATIVE COMMUNICATION

The assertion of parental authority in conflict with a child can encourage communication of a coercive kind. When this *coercive communication* occurs, commanding or conditional verbs are used: "ought," "should," "must," "will," "shall," or "you better." These verbs impose a point of view or course of action and limit discussion. Compare them to "want," "need," "wish," "may," "might," or "you could," words that signal a concern for the other person's point of view and lead the way to collaboration. Coercive communication can be condescending when the parent talks down to a child, and it often can feel threatening: "If you don't stop whining about this you'll be sorry!" Coercive communication is not open to information from the child. The child speaking up is treated as if she were talking back, the child complaining is treated as making excuses, the child questioning is treated as challenging, the child explaining is treated as arguing, the child disagreeing is treated as defying, the child criticizing is treated as attacking. A parent's coercive communication shuts the child's communication down.

Consider those blatant statements of authority that parents have made since time immemorial and that children resent, even when they consent:

- "Because I'm the parent, that's why!"
- "Because I make the rules, that's why!"
- "Because it's up to me, that's why!"
- "Just do what you're told!"
- "No talking back!"
- "No arguments!"
- "Understand!"

It's not that parents using coercive communication can't prevail. They can and usually do. And it's not that coercive communication by parents is not of some value. In an emergency, safety concerns must override the child's objections. "This is no time to argue, just do what I say!" But most of the time coercive use of authority can foreclose on communication by essentially saying to the child, "Don't give me any argument, just do what you're told." The informative value of conflict (using conflict as a talking point to better understand differences and how to work them out) is sacrificed in favor of the "instant gratification" of immediate compliance. Fortunately, coercive communication is only one way parents have to invoke their authority in conflict. There is another: *collaborative communication*. In both kinds of communication, parents can be determined to address the issue at disagreement, but each does so in very different ways. Parents using coercive communication *pull rank* on the child, declaring, "We are in charge. You have no say in the matter." On the other hand, parents who use collaborative communication *close ranks* with the child, declaring, "We will work out this problem together." Here is an example of how each style of authoritative communication might play out with a young child. Your daughter has stolen her best friend's expensive new toy, which the friend and her parents know is missing. You ask your child about her "new" possession, and she initially says, "Susie must have left it here." "Oh," you say, "I'll call her mother to let her know," "No!" she pleads, bursting into tears and admitting the truth: "Don't tell them that I took it! Susie will never want me to come over again and her parents will hate me!" Now what? What is the best way to handle this?

Coercively, you can dispose of the matter efficiently.

- "You did what?" (Interrogation)
- "You know that's wrong!" (Evaluation)
- "This is how you will deal with what you've done." (Direction)

Collaboratively, you might take a different tack.

- "What can you tell us about what you did and how you are feeling about it?" (Interrogation)
- "Let's talk about how what happened was not okay." (Evaluation)
- "We'll work with you to figure out how to make matters right." (Direction)

In a collaborative communication, the child is encouraged to ally with parental authority. With your help, your daughter realizes that it was wrong to take something that didn't belong to her and she comes up with her own words for a genuine apology. She also decides on a way to make amends to Susie and her parents, to restore good standing with them by providing some household service to them. Collaborative communication is concerned, empathetic, and supportive. In counseling, I encourage parents down the path of collaboration so that they can move quickly from conflict to communication. The parental commitments that mark this path, although not formally stated, include the following:

- "We respect our child enough to value the contribution of his point of view in helping us better understand and resolve this conflict between us."

- "We intend to listen to our child well enough to be able to state her point of view and position to her satisfaction."
- "We believe our child's opinion and self-interest are as important as our own."
- "No matter how opposed we are over this issue, we are committed to remaining on the same side, that of supporting the ongoing welfare of our relationship."
- "In support of that relationship, we intend to show concern for our child's feelings as we journey through this disagreement together."
- "The best resolution we can reach is one we all contribute to creating."

When parents take the initiative, willingness to collaborate quickly becomes mutual and the child usually signs on. Now parent and child are partners working out a common problem, not adversaries defending opposing interests.

I am *not* saying that parents should use their authority only collaboratively in conflict with their child, and never coercively. If there is a dangerous situation and the child is in opposition, coercive communication is what parents tend to use. On this occasion, they dictate action or firmness of purpose; they do not, at that moment, indulge in discussion. However, a collaborative approach is what works best to create mutual understanding and unity of purpose.

Another approach to noncoercive, collaborative communication is what psychologist Marshall Rosenberg calls "nonviolent communication." As he explains, nonviolent communication "is founded on language and communication skills that strengthen our ability to remain human even under trying conditions [interpersonal conflict being a major one].... We are led to express ourselves with honesty and clarity, while simultaneously paying others a respectful and empathetic attention."[4] In conflict, Rosenberg's approach is sensitive, collaborative, honest, specific, and solution-focused. For parents who are seeking an alternative to coercive communication, this program is well worth reading about.

It may initially be easier for women to accept a collaborative use of authority in conflict than men because of the different socialization that they receive in childhood.

SEXUAL DIFFERENCES IN CONFLICT

Men growing up in conflict with same-sex peers often learned to adopt a more coercive style of behavior because they derived self-esteem from performance, power, competition, and control. *Men are often trained to be dominant in conflict.* Therefore, in order to feel socially in charge, it may be important for a Dad to brook no disagreement from his child. So the child says, "I can't argue with my dad." Women growing up in conflict with same-sex peers often learned to adopt a more collaborative style because, for many women, relationship, empathy, communicating, and intimacy are what matters most. Female assertion of authority is often about keeping the contestants close. Thus in conflict with her child, it may be important for Mom to feel emotionally connected, to invite discussion. So the child says, "I can talk about anything with my mom." *Women are often trained to stay connected in conflict.*

In oversimplified terms, men are often trained to fight to win in conflict against each other, and women are often trained to try to understand each other in conflict. For this reason, dads tend to be quick to control the interaction and shut feelings down, while moms are more inclined to explore feelings as a way to become more sensitive and aware. Fathers can be more prone to treat the child as an *opponent*; mothers can be more prone to treat the child as an *informant*.

After reviewing research on sex differences in conflict, several psychologists cited studies suggesting that "men experience more negative arousal that takes longer periods to dissipate. Such arousal stems from different social experiences during childhood, in which women become accustomed to managing relational issues and men become more adept at activities, such as sports."[5] In my counseling experience I have found this distinction to hold true. Fathers tend to be the *performance-focused parent*, attending to actions and conduct (matters of doing), interests and mastery (matters of ability), and prowess and success (matters of achievement). Mothers tend to be the *relationship-focused parent*, attending to experience and emotion (matters of well-being), communication and intimacy (matters of staying connected), and esteem and happiness (matters of content). These differences often play out in how fathers and mothers interact in conflict with their children.

In conflict with his child, a dad's priorities might be to

- show dominance,
- speedily declare a resolution, and
- stop further emotional discomfort.

In conflict with her child, a mom's priorities might be to

- listen to what is being said,
- respond to what is being felt,
- work some resolution out together.

Certain types of risky behaviors that commonly occur in adolescence require the *combined* approaches that each parent has to give—paternal restraint declaring what needs to stop happening, and maternal communication opening up what needs to be talked about. Skipping school, sexual activity, or substance abuse, for example, all need to be countered by joint parental authority because the child's safety is at stake. The activity needs to be discouraged, but the choice and the thinking behind it need to be discussed and informed.

AUTHORITY AND CRACKING DOWN

When parents label a dangerous activity as rule breaking or wrongdoing and then apply some punitive consequence, this invocation of authority may be easy, but it can be insufficient. The errant child just pays the cost for the "crime" and then is free to offend again. Both parents and teenager may be relieved to get the issue "settled" and "over" and then move on. However, the additional commitment of *cracking down* is more effective than levying a consequence. By putting him on notice that henceforth they will want more communication and keeping closer tabs on his behavior, they let him know there is no "getting over" this episode. They will be factoring it into increased parental vigilance from here on out. They will remain more watchful, there will be more discussion, and some level of disagreement about this may be ongoing between them. "Cracking down" is the parents' way of saying

- "We will be reviewing your decisions more carefully."
- "We will be measuring out your freedom more cautiously."
- "We will be holding you more accountable for your conduct."
- "We will continue to talk with you about this kind of behavior."

This use of authority keeps the opportunity for conflict on this matter in play—as a topic for further discussion, as a point of increased supervision, and as a statement that they are ready and determined to respond should he choose to err the same way again.

Parents discover their teenager has had some episodes of substance use or abuse—alcohol or marijuana, for example. Immediately, they have two levels of concern—for the actual effects of the chemical on their adolescent (intended effects, side effects, interactive effects, and overdose) and for the dangerous choices made while under the influence that affect the teenager's functioning. Any psychoactive drug has the potential to alter the user's perception, thinking, judgment, mood, reactivity, and impulsiveness.

Parents fear at least *seven deadly experiences* that can damage or destroy children's lives, as follows:

- victimization from violence,
- accidental injury,
- school failure,
- illegal activities,
- sexual misadventures,
- suicidal despondency, and
- drug and alcohol involvement.

The last experience they fear is the most powerful of the seven because when you eliminate drug and alcohol involvement, you can reduce the incidence of the other six. *The choice to use substances affects how other life decisions are made.*[6]

Adolescence is fraught with risks from the desire to experience, to experiment with, and to explore more of life. Because substance abuse increases the jeopardy of that risk taking, parents can't be silent and leave the teenager's decisions on this matter unattended. As researchers note, "[T]oo little parental control over the teenager's decision making can lead to poor decisions if the teen lacks sufficient judgment skills to make mature, self-enhancing choices. The teenager may, through poor decision making, become involved in realistically dangerous situations with drugs, delinquency, alcohol, academic failure, and so forth, without the parents' awareness or concern."[7] Just because parents cannot literally *control* a teenager's choices does not mean they cannot *limit the opportunity* for those choices. Nor does it mean they cannot *inform* those choices with their own experience and understanding, and with outside help.

When parents discover that their child has had an episode of substance use or abuse, they need to take note, paying more attention to the day-to-day life choices their son or daughter is making. *A child who claims first-time use has usually used the substance before, just as a child who has started using is more likely to do so again.* In particular, when it comes to the drug that does most of the damage, *alcohol*, parents must take two contradictory but important stands in addition to increased surveillance. They must combine *prohibition* ("You do *not* have our blessing to drink and we will limit your freedom if we find you do drink") with *preparation* ("Should you still choose to drink, we want to talk about your drinking and some guidelines about how to have a safe drinking experience"). *Prohibition without preparation provides very limited protection.*

I believe all parents should be prepared to talk with their child about substance use and abuse starting in late elementary school, when adolescent interest in more grown-up activities begins. To the early and mid-adolescent, parents can explain why people use drugs, saying something like this about the most commonly used drug, alcohol: "Everyone, no matter the age, drinks for the same reason: for freedom. There is freedom from something negative and the desire for escape (from pain, for example), and there is freedom for something positive and the desire for indulgence (for feeling uninhibited, for example). The more intoxicated people become, the more their usual level of care about what they might do or say is lessened, until when they are drunk, they don't care at all. This is a very dangerous state to be in. I know movies and TV present people acting drunk as funny to watch and to be laughed at, but police would tell you that drunken decision making gets people into serious trouble—from carelessness and thoughtlessness, to confusion and aggression. You are now of an age when you will be hearing more about alcohol and drug use, and we would like you to tell us what you hear so we can talk about it and at least share what we know."

To the late adolescent, who is not yet of legal age to drink but is likely to have some social exposure and experimentation with drinking, parents need to give some instruction for evaluating personal use. You could say something like this: "Although you do not have our blessing to drink, should you choose to anyway, we want to give you some guidelines for safely managing your use.

- "Drink because you want to, not because you emotionally need to or socially feel you have to.
- "Drink so it only adds to life's pleasure and doesn't create any problems in your life.
- "Don't make drinking a habit so that you develop a dependency.
- "Don't drink to keep up with or compete with other people's drinking.
- "Don't drink to get drunk.
- "Don't drink so much that you can't exactly remember how much you drank.
- "Don't drink because everyone you know does it, but expand your social world to include friends who do not drink.
- "Don't drink because that's what friends always do for fun, but ask yourself if there are ways to have fun together that don't require drink.
- "Always ask yourself: 'What is my motivation for drinking and how could I satisfy that motivation differently?'
- "Don't drink to the point where your normal responsible care, judgment, perception, or decision making is affected in any negative or grandiose way.
- "Don't drink so much you end up making choices that you later regret.

- "Don't drink to medicate discomfort, fortify resolve, or escape from unhappiness.
- "Don't drink to the degree that it causes problems in the eyes of others.
- "Don't drink to the point that you find yourself denying, hiding, or lying about your use."

Because children grow up in a drug-filled world, every parent has to decide what to say to their adolescent about drinking and drugs, but it is not responsible to say nothing. *Substance use and abuse is not something to fight about with your child; it is something about which to talk to your adolescent honestly, openly, and continually.* Using the power of your personal experience in this discussion, using your informative authority, can be helpful.

INFORMATIVE AUTHORITY

Parental authority relies not just on having more positional power, but on having more *informative power*. Parents possess more knowledge about life from being older, wiser, and more experienced. As your adolescent enters the grown-up world, more interested in risk taking, your job is to continually *inform* his growing understanding with your own, using the authority of what you have seen and done to educate, advise, and warn.

All children are vicarious learners, using the experience of peers to educate themselves. They can also profit from the experience of parents. The question for these parents to ask themselves is this: "What have I learned from my own poor choices and hard experience that I could share with my growing child to spare her from making the same mistakes?" When parents share life lessons they learned from growing up, they become credible informants for their child. Rather than using a bad example for permission, "Well if you did then I can," children often decide to avoid a similar misadventure.

When a parent describes getting drunk at a party in high school, having indiscriminate sex and suffering harmful personal, social, and physical consequences, that information can have a powerfully preventive effect. "If I'd been sober, I would not have made the sexual decisions that I came to regret." The parent is speaking with enormous authority to children who know that the adult is not simply preaching, but teaching from painful personal experience. Now the child is in a receptive position to empathize and understand, not in an argumentative position to defend and fight. That is what I have seen in counseling.

THANKLESS CONFLICTS

Adolescence is about taking risks in order to grow. To moderate the dangers involved, parents need to use their rule-making authority and their informative authority to provide an understanding of risk taking. Sometimes parents must combat a child's reckless and self-destructive conduct when through substance abuse the young person could

- care less,
- act carelessly,
- care only about gratification, and
- not care about consequences at all.

Parents must use their authority to counter the effects of substance abuse, which can include skipping school to use drugs, and to insist on counseling to understand the needs that the drugs are being used to manage. They may have to fight for their child's life against his resistance. He doesn't want to attend school regularly (having fallen so far behind) and he would rather self-medicate than talk about his misery (which is painful for him). *Some of the most thankless conflicts occur when parents must use their protective authority for their child's best interests, confronting and treating a serious problem he wants them to ignore.* This is no time for parents to go it alone. They need to get the support of other parents who are experienced in dealing with such challenges. Going to the phone book and looking up the Toughlove or Al-Anon phone numbers to locate local meetings in their community is a good first step to find the company they need.

THREE IDEAS ABOUT *AUTHORITY AND CONFLICT* TO CARRY FORWARD

- Parental authority, no matter how commanding, never guarantees control, because compliance always depends on the child's cooperation; therefore parents must always work for their child's *consent*.
- Excessive reliance on coercive parental authority can only prevail at significant cost—the child's loss of safety, trust, honesty, and respect in the relationship, and at worst the loss of the child's love. So it behooves parents to use collaborative authority as often as they can.
- Because most children will intermittently test and contest their authority, parents must be prepared to engage in conflict over discipline to maintain a structure of safe and healthy family rules.

8

COMPROMISE AND CONFLICT

"When will the fighting stop?" weary parents ask each other, longing for peace and quiet, "Why can't everyone just get along?" This is an important question because the answer shows that conflict is built into all human relationships in which there is a significant degree of interdependence (reliance on each other) and caring (valuing of each other), or both, as occurs in families. At best, such relationships prove to be potentially contentious arrangements because a mix of three experiences must be continually compromised as everyone adjusts to changes within each other, between each other, and in circumstances around each other, in order to get along.

COMPROMISE IN RELATIONSHIPS

A successful compromise is based on a mix of three experiences that characterize all committed relationships.

- Each person seeks *benefits*—interpersonal rewards in the relationship of pleasure and fulfillment that one wants to give and to receive. The parent wants to give love and receive appreciation, for example, and the child wants to offer accomplishment and receive approval.
- Each person accepts *limits*—interpersonal costs in the relationship, the sacrifice or curtailing of personal freedom out of a sense of responsibility

and obligation to each other. The parent must support but not over-indulge the child, for example, and the child must be honest but must not be rude.

- Each person endures *hurt*—interpersonal risks of injury, mostly unintentional and insensitive, arising from acts of omission and commission, what the other person neglects to do or unmindfully proceeds to do. There are hurts to the child when a parent forgets a promise or is excessively demanding, for example, and hurts to the parent when the child doesn't listen to instructions or accidentally breaks what he was told not to use.

The compromise that everyone in the family must learn to live with is "some." Some benefits will have to be enough, some limits will have to be accepted, and some hurts will have to be endured. The reason everyone can't "just get along" is this: Not only do people never get all the benefits from a relationship they want all the time; there are no "benefits only" relationships any more than there is "free" love in a committed adult relationship. Some limits and hurts are part of the package. The best working compromise any family member can realistically hope for is a relationship in which there are maximum benefits, moderate limits, and minimal hurts. For a domineering parent or a willful child this concept of compromise can be hard to accept since they want everything their way and object when it is not. Less than full benefits can seem unjust, limits on personal freedom can feel intolerable, and any experience of hurt can feel unbearable—particularly for people who refuse to let hurt go.

In family counseling, I continually see this combustible mix of the three experiences explode into conflict when family members

- fight for benefits they believe they deserve,
- fight against limits they believe are too restrictive,
- fight to defend themselves from further hurt or retaliate for hurt received.

Part of my job in counseling is to help a parent and child reach a workable compromise. My objective is to increase sensitivity and encourage respect so that each might say to the other: "I know what parts of our relationship you value most highly. I know what sacrifices you find most difficult to make. And I know where you are most vulnerable to feeling hurt." How well they treat each other depends in large measure on how well they know each other and how willing they are to respect the wants, needs, and vulnerabilities of the other that they have come to understand.

The complex process of establishing a working compromise is movingly illustrated by a teenager's first love, where the idealization of romance and passion collides with the hard reality of relationship. There are frustrating disagreements about what is *enough*. There are benefit conflicts: What is enough personal time together and enough social time apart? There are limit conflicts: How much is enough personal disclosure and what is each person's right to privacy? There are hurt conflicts: How much anger is it okay to express and what is too much? Parents often wonder why their smitten adolescent is so frequently unhappy. These conflicts are particularly difficult to manage in the blush of new love, when feelings are so strong and so fragile.

COMPROMISE IS CHALLENGING FOR EVERYONE IN THE FAMILY

For one person to get a benefit, the other person's benefit may have to be delayed or denied. So a parent settles a conflict between siblings over use of the computer by requiring them to "take turns," which keeps one child happily occupied while the other one smolders. One child may feel jealous on his sibling's birthday, resenting how his brother or sister is getting all the attention. When one person gets a benefit, another must accept a limit. The child who gets a ride to soccer practice every weekday after school enjoys a benefit that imposes a limitation on his mother the chauffeur, who on some days would rather be doing something else. When one person gets a benefit, another may feel hurt or deprived. When an eight-year-old has a friend over and the parent tells her six-year-old sister to leave the playmates alone, the younger child feels left out. One parent gets to travel to a glamorous destination on business, and the other stays home with the added stress of doing both his own job during the day and single parenting at night. Conflict tends to arise when the current mix in a relationship is no longer workable for one person. Her benefits feel too few, her sacrifices too great, and the hurt too deep. When this happens, it helps to ask these questions:

- "How can we manage the mix of experiences so we all get along as well as possible?"
- "How can we repair relationships when we haven't been getting along because the compromise has become unworkable?"

To answer these questions we must be identify the four levels of family conflict.

THE FOUR LEVELS OF FAMILY CONFLICT

The four levels of family conflict, in order of severity, are as follows:

- level one: the inability to discuss compromise,
- level two: living with a bad bargain,
- level three: the onset of chronic complaints, and
- level four: the beginning of long-term damage.

Level one: The inability to discuss compromise. What the parent knows—and what the young child must through daily experience come to accept—is that in a good compromise each person gets some benefits, accepts some limits, and doesn't experience too much hurt. Ideally, the benefits of the relationship will outweigh the sacrifice of limits and the discomfort of hurts most of the time. So even though a parent can be grouchy, tired, or distracted at the end of a long day, and not that much fun to be around, *for the most part* the child finds the relationship affirming and rewarding. Although a two-year-old can often be obstinate and upset, *for the most part* parents find her to be cooperative and companionable. "For the most part" has to be good enough. That is the meaning of compromise.

When either parent or child is going through a sustained period of discontent, however, the parent needs to question the current compromise. It may be time to renegotiate and modify the mix. Sometimes a family change has altered the mix for the worse but neither the parent nor the child has communicated their feelings about the result. At the birth of a second child, the parents may become absorbed in infant care, while the first child, feeling dethroned and neglected, experiences reduced benefits (less parental attention), increased limits (directives to be quiet because the baby is sleeping), and more hurt (from the feeling that she has been supplanted in their love). In this case, the parents may need to *restore* attention, *relax* the restrictions on the older child, and take the time to *reassure* her that they still love her as much as ever.

What parents should *not* do is ignore the warning signs of sustained unhappiness on the child's side or their own. When they don't talk about how the compromise is becoming unacceptable and decide to let it carry on, they set up a more serious level of conflict as everyone learns to live with what becomes a bad bargain in the relationship between them.

Level two: Living with a bad bargain. When either parents or child know a level one mix is not working, why would they decline to discuss the dissatisfaction or unhappiness they feel?

- Perhaps they don't want to bring it up and cause a problem.
- Perhaps they feel foolish, selfish, or anxious about appearing to complain.
- Perhaps they want to avoid an argument.
- Perhaps they hope the situation will improve on its own.

When feelings of discontent go unexpressed, frustration and irritation keep building until the unhappy party reaches a boiling point and explodes: "I have given up all this freedom, I have endured all this hurt, and I do not receive sufficient benefits to make my sacrifice worthwhile!" The relationship has become a bad bargain and the offended party wants it to change. The stage for level two conflict is now set.

So parents explode at the fifth-grader who promised to do his homework if they would just stop bugging him about it, a compromise to which they agreed, only to discover that they had made a bad bargain when the teacher calls about the two weeks' worth of missing assignments. "We give you the responsibility you say you wanted, and this is what we get in return?" Or the junior in high school has silently lived with her demanding parent's dissatisfaction long enough and vows to take it no longer: "All you ever do is criticize! However well I do is never good enough! It's always been this way! No matter how hard I try, I can never please you!"

A compromise that doesn't work for one party and is allowed to continue soon becomes what I term a bad bargain. It feels like the efforts made do not provide an adequate return. And when a bad bargain goes unchallenged for too long without the aggrieved party communicating his displeasure, bad feelings fester. Now, instead of just needing to negotiate a new, more equitable compromise, the parties must deal with the costs of grievance. At the bad bargain point, the injured party is going to need some empathetic listening before he will be willing to talk about a compromise. The child who broke his word about taking responsibility for doing his homework will have to listen to his parents describe the emotional price they have paid for misplaced trust. The demanding parent is going to have to listen to a painful description of how his unrelenting criticism has injured his teenage child over the years. *To resolve level two conflicts, parent and child must first hear all grievances out.* A bad bargain should never be allowed to stand.

Level three: The onset of chronic complaints. If parent and child do not speak up to address their unhappiness with the level one compromise, and if they refuse to confront the grievance that has built up in level two, then they begin to burden their relationship with more intransigent conflicts on level three. They start bickering, exchanging chronic complaints. Whereas conflict at the bad bargain point included confiding grievances, level three conflict deals in *accusations.* The following are typical:

- Inadequate benefits. "My wants are consistently unmet, this relationship is not worthwhile."
- Excessive limits. "I have given up too much for this relationship. It's not fair!"
- Ongoing hurts. "You keep harming me. This relationship is painful."

It is important to recognize the destructive power of constant complaining. Criticism from complaints injures the other party emotionally and polarizes the relationship as each side settles into the role of accused or accuser or, sometimes, both. Criticism easily devolves into name-calling as each person labels the other with a derogatory stereotype: "You are so lazy! How can you be so irresponsible?" In counseling, level three conflict is easy to identify because of such insults, which do not encourage compromise, but increase resistance to it.

Level three conflict is common during the mid-adolescent passage, especially between the ages of thirteen and fifteen. By this time the discontent, resistance, and limit testing of early adolescence have done their disaffecting work, having worn down the good feeling at home. Parent and early adolescent love each other as much as ever, but they often don't like each other as well as when they were parent and child.

Ironically, at this point in their relationship, parent and mid-adolescent often share common complaints against each other.

- "You never appreciate all that I do!"
- "You're never satisfied with what I give!"
- "You're always after me for something more!"
- "You're always busy when I need you now!"
- "You're always acting irritated and upset!"
- "You treat others better than you treat me!"

Parent and child should not passively accept these complaints as uncorrectable. They should instead listen to them and use them as the basis for bettering their relationship. The parent may not have realized that his child felt unappreciated, and can decide to show his appreciation more. The mid-adolescent may offer to help more to show consideration. They may both agree to spend more recreational time together. Chronic complaints only get worse when allowed to stand, begetting a grudging attitude and lack of effort that set up the likelihood of serious damage to the relationship over time. "If that's the way you're going to be, then why try?"

Level four: The beginning of long-term damage. Treating discontent as a terminal condition, both parties give up on the possibility of improvement. They start disliking each other and diminish their efforts to get along. Whereas conflict at the level of normal compromise generates *dissatisfactions*, conflict at the bad bargain point generates *grievances*, and conflict at the point of chronic complaints generates *accusations*, level four conflict generates deep *resentments*. Here long-term damage can be done unless an exchange of mutual benefits can be restored, bearable limits reset, and acting to hurt each other relinquished.

Level four conflicts commonly occur in families where extreme circumstantial change discourages adequate communication at the time. The urgency of meeting new demands takes precedence over discussing unhappiness that necessary adjustments cause. "Not now, we don't have time to talk about it," a recently divorced single parent tells her children whom she has to move from a larger living space into a small apartment by the end of the next week. By the time they get in, and before they are settled, in her words, "Nobody wants anything to do with anyone, everyone is angry, and being mean to each other seems to be the best that the children can do." Welcome to level four.

Ideally, dissatisfactions experienced by the children would have been discussed when the prospect of the move arose, but crises often make conditions in families less than ideal for adequate communication. So when the children experienced discontent with the move on level one, it was ignored. Allowed to build up to grievance in level two, it remained unspoken. Voiced as complaints on level three, they were not corrected. And now, come level four, the single parent finally stops long enough to quell resentments and prevent the likelihood of long-term damage. Amid the disarray of unpacked boxes, she sits them all down so they can hear everybody out and then begins to reconstruct their relationships, forging what working compromise she can. She helps identify benefits everyone has missed (having time for family play with her at night), she discusses reasonable new limits for all of them to live by (reinstating some of the old schedule of household help they gave before), and she talks about treating each other well (not taking out bad feelings by treating each other badly as has been going on). "We're not just a new family anymore," she says. "We are a new team, and we have to work together so that the family works for us all."

HOW CONFLICTS WORSENS

Parents are not in the business of eliminating conflict, but they are in the business of keeping it within constructive bounds. This is why monitoring the level of family conflict is important. Remember:

- Shut up on level one.
- Build up on level two.
- Harden up on level three.
- Give up on level four.

This is how conflict destroys relationships.

In general, parent and child need to keep their conflicts on levels one and two, confronting unworkable compromises and addressing bad bargains when dissatisfaction over some aspect of their relationship has been ignored or put off. Once their conflict descends to levels three and four, chronic complaints and long-term damage, recovery and resolution can take a lot of time and energy and work. *I believe it is the parent's job to monitor conflict in the family and to do all they can to keep it confined to the first two levels.*

"Why can't we just have peace in the family?" parents ask. They can, but they must define the word "peace" realistically. Peaceful families are *not* families without conflict. They are families in which family members mostly resolve their conflicts on level one. They accept and work with the compromise of their experience with each other, as best as they can; the ever-changing mix of benefits and limits and hurts is simply part of their relationship.

THREE IDEAS ABOUT
COMPROMISE AND CONFLICT
TO CARRY FORWARD

- The ability for parent and child to have a harmonious relationship is the outcome of a working compromise between three essential experiences in their relationship: *benefits* that each party wants, *limits* that each party accepts, and *hurts* that each party must occasionally endure.

- Intermittent conflict is required to address and redress this compromise when it stops working for one or both parties.
- To ignore, deny, or avoid an unworkable compromise is to invite a worsening conflict between parent and child that gets harder to resolve over time.

CONCLUSION

What do I hope you have concluded by reading this book? It is that conflict is a necessary process for confronting, discussing, and resolving inevitable differences between family members. It is that the objectives of healthy conflict are to increase mutual understanding of differences between each other, and to strengthen the relationship by creating a resolution both parties are committed to support. It is that one responsibility of parents, through instruction, interaction, and example, is to teach children and adolescents constructive ways to disagree. And finally, it is to recognize that one doesn't stop a conflict by fighting to end it. One ends a conflict by agreeing to stop the fighting and stop the screaming.

APPENDIX A

BEHAVIORS TO AVOID IN FAMILY CONFLICT

Teaching children how to manage conflict is an act of *commission* when parents model constructive behavior. It is also an act of *omission* because parents must be careful not to engage in destructive behavior. What are some destructive behaviors to avoid? I found the beginnings of such a list in a very helpful book about living with someone who has borderline personality disorder, *Stop Walking on Eggshells*.[1] Here is my list describing some of what *not* to do in family conflict, including many suggestions derived from *Stop Walking on Eggshells*.

- Do not manipulate the other person with lies to influence the outcome of a disagreement.
- Do not extort an agreement from the other person by threatening to have negative feelings or by promising to have positive feelings only if you get your way.
- Do not treat the other person as all right one minute and all wrong the next, with no room in between.
- Do not treat your needs as all important and the other person's needs as unimportant.
- Do not blame the other person for being demanding, causing problems, or having something wrong with her because she has dared to disagree with you.

- Do not make unilateral decisions about what the other person is thinking, feeling, or intending, but respect her authority for truly knowing her own inner state.
- Do not belittle or deny the other person's viewpoint just because it is different from your own.
- Do not use words or actions in conflict that you know will cause the other person pain.
- Do not use threats or threatening actions to bully the other person to acquiesce or avoid conflict with you out of fear of getting hurt.
- Do not deliberately distort the meaning of what the other person has said and use it against him in this or another conflict later.
- Do not blame the conflict on the other person when it was you who was looking for a fight.
- Do not seesaw back and forth between loving and raging feelings to keep the other person off balance with anxiety at your unpredictability.
- Do not insist that the other person is always wrong and can never do anything right.
- Do not accuse the other person of doing or saying things you know he didn't do or say.
- Do not use sarcasm or ridicule, or otherwise put down the other person for speaking up.
- Do not act to prevent the other person, who has said he is feeling frustrated or unsafe, from taking a time-out or from leaving the scene of the conflict until you have had your say or gotten your way.
- Do not make excuses for your destructive behavior or try to make the other person believe that your harmful behavior didn't happen, that everything's all right.
- Do not treat disagreement with you as evidence that the other person is automatically in the wrong.
- Do not treat expression of your temper as okay in conflict so long as you get your way.
- Do not use conflict to get even with or to get revenge on the other person.

APPENDIX B

A CODE OF FAMILY CONFLICT

Years ago, I wrote the "Code of Family Conflict," by which I still stand.

> HOW ONE BEHAVES IN CONFLICT
> DEPENDS ON THE NATURE OF THE RELATIONSHIP
> BECAUSE AT OPPOSITE EXTREMES
> FIGHTING WITH A PERSON ONE LOVES
> NEEDS TO BE CONDUCTED DIFFERENTLY
> FROM DOING BATTLE AGAINST AN ENEMY IN WAR.
>
> IF CARING FOR THE OTHER PERSON
> MEANS A LOT,
> THEN THE MEANS
> (HOW PEOPLE TREAT EACH OTHER IN CONFLICT)
> BECOMES MORE IMPORTANT THAN THE END
> (THE RESOLUTION REACHED)
> BECAUSE PRESERVATION OF THAT CARING
> WILL DETERMINE FUTURE HAPPINESS TOGETHER.

IN WAR,

THE RELATIONSHIP BE DAMNED.

SINCE THE ENEMY IS OUT TO KILL,

ANY MEANS OF COMBAT JUSTIFIES THE END,

WHICH IS SELF-DEFENSE AND WINNING AT ALL COSTS.

UNHAPPILY, SOMETIMES INSTEAD OF KEEPING FAITH WITH LOVE

WHEN OPPOSITION ARISES AND ARGUMENT BREAKS OUT,

A FAMILY MEMBER

(WHO WAS "ATTACK TRAINED" GROWING UP)

SUBSTITUTES THE TACTICS OF WAR

AND AROUSED BY EMOTIONAL INTENSITY

ACTS TO VIOLATE THE PRIMARY RULE FOR FAMILY CONFLICT: *SAFETY.*

WHILE DIFFERENCES ARE UNAVOIDABLE

AND CONFLICT IS INEVITABLE,

VIOLENCE IS NEITHER.

IT IS A MATTER OF CHOICE.

THEREFORE,

CHOOSE A CODE OF CONDUCT THAT DECREES:

"CONFLICT SHALL NEVER BE AN ACCEPTABLE CAUSE

FOR INFLICTING INJURY ON ANOTHER FAMILY MEMBER."

"WELL, I ONLY DID THAT TO SHOW WHO WAS IN CHARGE!"

"WELL, I ONLY SAID THAT BECAUSE I WAS SO ANGRY!"

THESE EXPLANATIONS ARE NO GOOD EXCUSE.

AUTHORITY AND ANGER NEED TO FIND A SAFER WAY.

ALTHOUGH ASSAULTING THE ENEMY HAS MILITARY USE,

IN FAMILY CONFLICT THIS BEHAVIOR CONSTITUTES ABUSE.[1]

APPENDIX C

IN CASE OF VIOLENCE

The family conflicts I describe in this book stop short of being the abusive or violent kind. However, all conflict has this injurious potential if it escalates to an extreme degree. Should this unhappy experience occur in your home, it is important that you get outside help for immediate restraint and for emotional recovery. Call your local police department to report a family disturbance. For support and additional advice, you can also call the National Domestic Violence Hotline, 1 800 799 SAFE (7233). *The longer repeated incidents of abusive or violent conflict go unreported in your family, the greater the likelihood that they will continue and the worse they are likely to become.* After such an incident occurs, get some family counseling in order to repair and heal injured relationships.

NOTES

INTRODUCTION

1. Daniel J. Canary, William R. Cupach, and Susan J. Messman, *Relationship Conflict: Conflict in Parent-Child, Friendship, and Romantic Relationships* (Thousand Oaks, CA: SAGE, 1995), p. xii.
2. Dudley Weeks, *The Eight Essential Steps to Conflict Resolution* (New York: Tarcher/Penguin, 1994), p. 4.

1 COOPERATION AND CONFLICT

1. Daniel J. Canary, William R. Cupach, and Susan J. Messman, *Relationship Conflict: Conflict in Parent-Child, Friendship, and Romantic Relationships* (Thousand Oaks, CA: SAGE, 1995), p. 3.
2. David C. Hall, *Stop Arguing and Start Understanding: Eight Steps to Solving Family Conflicts* (Seattle, WA: Montlake Family Press, 2001), p. 26.
3. "Hidden Kitchens: The Kitchen Sisters," National Public Radio, KUT, Austin, Texas, November 22, 2007.
4. Hall, *Stop Arguing*, p. 17.
5. Ethan Bronner, "Books of the Times," *The New York Times*, April 16, 2008, p. B8.
6. Dudley Weeks, *The Eight Essential Steps to Conflict Resolution* (New York: Tarcher/Penguin, 1994), p. 247.

2 EMOTION AND CONFLICT

1. Sandra Graham and Valerie S. Folkes, *Attribution Theory: Applications to Achievement, Mental Health, and Interpersonal Conflict* (Hillside, NJ: Lawrence Erlbaum Associates, 1990), p. 172.
2. Daniel J. Canary, William R. Cupach, and Susan J. Messman, *Relationship Conflict: Conflict in Parent-Child, Friendship, and Romantic Relationships* (Thousand Oaks, CA: SAGE, 1995), p. 18.

3. Claude Steiner, with Paul Perry, *Achieving Emotional Literacy: A Personal Program to Increase Emotional Literacy* (New York: Avon, 1997), p. 29.
4. Daniel Goleman, *Emotional Intelligence: Why It Can Matter More Than IQ* (New York: Bantam, 1995), p. 28.
5. Sandra Aamodt and Sam Wang, "Exercise on the Brain," *New York Times*, November 8, 2007, p. A31.
6. Goleman, *Emotional Intelligence*, p. 32.
7. Steven P. Shelov and Robert E. Hanneman, *Caring for Your Baby and Young Child* (New York: Bantam, American Academy of Pediatrics, 2005), pp. 525–6.
8. Steiner, *Achieving Emotional Literacy*, p. 25.
9. Linda Sonna, *The Everything ® Toddler Book* (Avon, MA: Adams Media, 2002), p. 158.
10. Goleman, *Emotional Intelligence*, pp. 158–9.
11. Carl E. Pickhardt, *The Everything® Parent's Guide to the Strong-Willed Child* (Avon, MA: Adams Media, 2005), p. 173.
12. Carl E. Pickhardt, *Keys to Successful Stepfathering* (Hauppauge, NY: Barron's, 1997), pp. 124–8.
13. Canary et al., *Relationship Conflict*, p. 46.
14. John Narciso and David Burkett, *Relating Redefined: Discovering the New "Language" for Communicating* (San Antonio, TX: Redman-Wright, 1992), p. 21.
15. Carl E. Pickhardt, *Keys to Single Parenting* (Hauppauge, NY: Barron's, 1996), p. 29.
16. Susan Forward, *Emotional Blackmail: When People in Your Life Use Fear, Obligation, and Guilt to Manipulate You* (New York: HarperCollins, 1997), p. x.

3 COMMUNICATION AND CONFLICT

1. Carl E. Pickhardt, *The Connected Father: Understanding Your Unique Role and Responsibilities during Your Child's Adolescence* (New York: Palgrave Macmillan, 2007), pp. 163–4.
2. John Narciso and David Burkett, *Relating Redefined: Discovering the New "Language" for Communicating* (San Antonio, TX: Redman-Wright, 1992), p. 7.
3. Ibid. 17.
4. Sandra Graham and Valerie S. Folkes, *Attribution Theory: Applications to Achievement, Mental Health, and Interpersonal Conflict* (Hillsdale, NJ: Lawrence Erlbaum Associates, 1990), p. 207.

5. Friederich Forsterling, *Attribution: An Introduction to Theories, Research and Applications* (Philadelphia, PA: Taylor & Francis, 2001), p. 91.
6. Fraser Harbour Hodder, "Cognitive Biases: Willing to War," *Harvard Magazine*, May–June 2007, p. 15.
7. Dudley Weeks, *The Eight Essential Steps to Conflict Resolution* (New York: Tarcher/Penguin, 1994), p. 124.

4 INTOLERANCE AND CONFLICT

1. Marilyn B. Brewer, "The Importance of Being We: Human Nature and Intergroup Relations," *American Psychologist*, 62, no. 8 (2007), 729.
2. T. S. Eliot, *The Complete Plays of T.S. Eliot* (New York: Harcourt, Brace & World, 1963), p. 110.
3. Dudley Weeks, *The Eight Essential Steps to Conflict Resolution* (New York: Tarcher/Penguin, 1994), pp. 33–4.
4. Darrell Sifford, *The Only Child* (New York: Harper & Row, 1990), p. 170.
5. Arthur L. Robin and Sharon L. Foster, *Negotiating Parent-Adolescent Conflict* (New York: Guilford Press, 1989), pp. 29–30.
6. Bob Dylan, "The Times They Are A-changin'" (©1963, renewed 1991, Special Rider).
7. Carl E. Pickhardt, *The Connected Father: Understanding Your Unique Role and Responsibilities during Your Child's Adolescence* (New York: Palgrave Macmillan, 2007), p. 201.
8. Gary Harper, *The Joy of Conflict Resolution* (Gabriola Island, BC: New Society, 2004), p. 129.
9. Pickhardt, *Connected Father*, p. 177.
10. Joshua Coleman, *When Parents Hurt—Compassionate Strategies When You and Your Grown Child Don't Get Along* (New York: HarperCollins, 2007), p. 96.
11. Carl E. Pickhardt, *Keys to Successful Stepfathering* (Hauppauge, NY: Barron's, 1997), pp. 46–8.
12. Carl E. Pickhardt, *The Future of Your Only Child* (New York: Palgrave Macmillan, 2008), pp. 119–20.

5 RESEMBLANCE AND CONFLICT

1. Hara Estroff Marano, "Unconventional Wisdom," *Psychology Today*, March/April 2008, p. 51.

2. David C. Hall, *Stop Arguing and Start Understanding: Eight Steps to Solving Family Conflicts* (Seattle, WA: Montlake Family Press, 2001), p. 105.
3. Marano, "Unconventional Wisdom," p. 51.
4. Tara Parker-Pope, "In Sisters, Love and the Urge to Wring Her Neck," *The New York Times,* Science Times, March 18, 2008, p. D5.
5. Adele Faber and Elaine Mazlish, *Siblings without Rivalry: How to Help Your Children Live Together So You Can Live Too* (New York: W.W. Norton, 1987), p. 14.
6. Parker-Pope, "In Sisters," p. D5.

6 CHANGE AND CONFLICT

1. Steven P. Shelov and Robert E. Hanneman, *Caring for Your Baby and Young Child* (New York: Bantam, American Academy of Pediatrics, 2005), p. 538.
2. Jean Walbridge, ACSW, LCSW, "On Lying in Adolescence," 2006, www.parentingadolescents.com.
3. "Web Reaches New Milestone: 100 Million Sites," CNN.com Technology, November 1, 2006.
4. Harlan Coben, "The Undercover Parent: Why It's O.K. to Spy on Your Children," *The New York Times,* Sunday Opinion, March 16, 2008, p. WK14.

7 AUTHORITY AND CONFLICT

1. Billy Mutschler, "Human Beings," *The Dime Store Poets*, Electric Rhymes (© 2005 Billy Mutschler), BMI.
2. Arthur L. Robin and Sharon L. Foster, *Negotiating Parent-Adolescent Conflict* (New York: Guilford Press, 1989), p. 22.
3. Hara Estroff Marano, "Unconventional Wisdom," *Psychology Today*, March/April 2008, p. 51.
4. Marshall B. Rosenberg, *Nonviolent Communication: A Language of Compassion* (Encinitas, CA: PuddleDancer, 1999), pp. 3–4.
5. Daniel J. Canary, William R. Cupach, and Susan J. Messman, *Relationship Conflict: Conflict in Parent-Child, Friendship, and Romantic Relationships* (Thousand Oaks, CA: SAGE, 1995), p. 132.
6. Carl E. Pickhardt, *Keys to Raising a Drug-Free Child* (Hauppauge, NY: Barron's Educational Series, 1999), p. vii.
7. Robin and Foster, *Negotiating Parent-Adolescent Conflict*, p. 22.

APPENDIX A: BEHAVIORS TO
AVOID IN FAMILY CONFLICT

1. Paul T. Mason and Randi Kreger, *Stop Walking on Eggshells: Taking Back Your Life When Someone You Care About Has Borderline Personality Disorder* (Oakland, CA: New Harbinger, 1998), pp. 11–13.

APPENDIX B: A CODE OF FAMILY CONFLICT

1. Carl E. Pickhardt, *The Meaning of Masks: A Psychological Journey* (Philadelphia, PA: Xlibris, 2002), p. 107.

FURTHER READING

Aamodt, Sandra, and Sam Wang. "Exercise on the Brain." *New York Times*, November 8, 2007, A31.

Bancroft, Lundy. *Why Does He Do That? Inside the Minds of Angry and Controlling Men*. New York: Berkley Books, 2002.

Brazelton, T. Berry, and Joshua D. Sparrow. *Understanding Sibling Rivalry, the Brazelton Way*. Cambridge, MA: De Capo Lifelong, 2005.

Brewer, Marilyn B. "The Importance of Being 'We': Human Nature and Intergroup Relations." *American Psychologist* 62, no. 8 (2007): 728–38.

Brody, Jane E. "Personal Health: Teenage Risks and How to Avoid Them." *New York Times*, Science Times, December 18, 2007, D7.

Canary, Daniel J., William R. Cupach, and Susan J. Messman. *Relationship Conflict: Conflict in Parent-Child, Friendship, and Romantic Relationships*. Thousand Oaks, CA: SAGE, 1995.

Coben, Harlan. "The Undercover Parent: Why It's O.K. to Spy on Your Children." *New York Times*, Sunday Opinion, Week in Review, March 16, 2008, 14.

Coleman, Joshua. *When Parents Hurt: Compassionate Strategies When You and Your Grown Child Don't Get Along*. New York: HarperCollins, 2007.

Dylan, Bob. "The Times They Are A-changin'." ©1963, renewed 1991 Special Rider.

Eisenberg, Arlene, Heidi E. Murkoff, and Sandee E. Hathaway. *What to Expect: The Toddler Years*. New York: Workman, 1996.

Eliot, T. S. *The Complete Plays of T. S. Eliot*. New York: Harcourt, Brace & World, 1963.

Evans, Patricia. *The Verbally Abusive Relationship*. Avon, MA: Adams Media, 1992.

Faber, Adele, and Elaine Mazlish. *Siblings without Rivalry: How to Help Your Children Live Together So You Can Live Too*. New York: W.W. Norton, 1987.

Forsterling, Friederich. *Attribution: An Introduction to Theories, Research and Applications*. Philadelphia, PA: Taylor & Francis, 2001.

Forward, Susan. *Emotional Blackmail: When People in Your Life Use Fear, Obligation, and Guilt to Manipulate You*. New York: HarperCollins, 1997.

Goleman, Daniel. *Emotional Intelligence: Why It Can Matter More Than IQ*. New York: Bantam, 1995.

Graham, Sandra, and Valerie S. Folkes. *Attribution Theory: Applications to Achievement, Mental Health, and Interpersonal Conflict*. Hillside, NJ: Lawrence Erlbaum Associates, 1990.

Hall, David C. *Stop Arguing and Start Understanding: Eight Steps to Solving Family Conflicts*. Seattle, WA: Montlake Family Press, 2001.

Harper, Gary. *The Joy of Conflict Resolution*. Gabriola Island, BC, Canada: New Society, 2004.

Haxton, Brooks. *Fragments: The Collected Wisdom of Heraclitus*. New York: Penguin Putnam, 2001.

Hodder, Fraser Harbour. "Cognitive Biases: Willing to War." *Harvard Magazine*, May–June 2007, 15–16.

Marano, Hara Estroff. "Unconventional Wisdom." *Psychology Today*, March–April 2008, 51.

Mason, Paul T., and Randi Kreger. *Stop Walking on Eggshells: Taking Back Your Life When Someone You Care About Has Borderline Personality Disorder*. Oakland, CA: New Harbinger, 1998.

Mock, Douglas W. *More Than Kin and Less Than Kind: The Evolution of Family Conflict*. Cambridge, MA: The Belknap Press of Harvard University Press, 2004.

Murkoff, Heidi, Arlene Eisenberg, and Sandee Hathaway. *What to Expect the First Year*. New York: Workman, 2003.

Myers, Alyse. "How I Met My Mother." *New York Times Magazine*, May 11, 2008, 86.

Narciso, John, and David Burkett. *Relating Redefined: Discovering the New "Language" for Communicating*. San Antonio, TX: Redman-Wright, 1992.

Parker-Pope, Tara. "In Sisters, Love and an Urge to Wring Her Neck." *New York Times*, Science Times, March 18, 2008, D5.

Pettus, Ashley. "A Spectrum of Disorders: The Urgent Need to Understand the Biological Basis of Autism." *Harvard Magazine*, January/February 2008, 27.

Pickhardt, Carl E. *The Connected Father: Understanding Your Unique Role and Responsibilities during Your Child's Adolescence*. New York: Palgrave Macmillan, 2007.

———. *The Everything® Parent's Guide to Children and Divorce*. Avon, MA: Adams Media, 2006.

———. *The Everything® Parent's Guide to Positive Discipline*. Avon, MA: Adams Media, 2004.

———. *The Everything® Parent's Guide to the Strong-Willed Child*. Avon, MA: Adams Media, 2005.

———. *From Cell to Society*. Boston, MA: Houghton Mifflin, 1965. Republished, Lincoln, NE: iUniverse, 2001.

———. *The Future of Your Only Child*. New York: Palgrave Macmillan, 2008.

————. *Keys to Raising a Drug-free Child*. Hauppauge, NY: Barron's, 1999.

————. *Keys to Single Parenting*. Hauppauge, NY: Barron's, 1996.

————. *Keys to Successful Stepfathering*. Hauppauge, NY: Barron's, 1997.

————. *The Meaning of Masks: A Psychological Journey*. Philadelphia, PA: Xlibris, 2002.

————. *PSYMBOLS: Logos for the Mind*. Philadelphia, PA: Xlibris, 2005.

Pinker, Steven. *How the Mind Works*. New York: Norton, 1997.

Pollan, Michael. "Our Decrepit Food Factories." *New York Times Sunday Magazine*, December 16, 2007, 25.

Robin, Arthur L., and Sharon L. Foster. *Negotiating Parent-Adolescent Conflict*. New York: Guilford Press, 1989.

Rosenberg, Marshall B. *Nonviolent Communication: A Language of Compassion*. Encinitas, CA: PuddleDancer, 1999.

Saltus, Richard. *Broken Symmetry*, Howard Hughes Medical Institute Bulletin 20, no. 3 (August 2007): 28.

Sears, William, and Martha Sears. *The Fussy Baby Book*. New York: Little, Brown, 1996.

Shelov, Steven P. *Your Baby's First Year*. New York: Bantam Dell, American Academy of Pediatrics, 2005.

Shelov, Steven P., and Robert E. Hanneman. *Caring for Your Baby and Young Child*. New York: Bantam, American Academy of Pediatrics, 2005.

Sifford, Darrell. *The Only Child*. New York: Harper & Row, 1990.

Sonna, Linda. *The Everything® Toddler Book*. Avon, MA: Adams Media, 2002.

Steiner, Claude, with Paul Perry. *Achieving Emotional Literacy: A Personal Program to Increase Emotional Literacy*. New York: Avon, 1997.

Sulloway, Frank J. *Born to Rebel: Birth Order, Family Dynamics, and Creative Lives*. New York: Vintage, 1997.

Walbridge, Jean, ACSW, LCSW. "On Lying in Adolescence." http://www.parentingadolescents.com (2006).

Weeks, Dudley. *The Eight Essential Steps to Conflict Resolution*. New York: Tarcher/Penguin, 1994.

INDEX